C000301327

TOWARDS 2000

Edited by

Liz Wakefield

First published in Great Britain in 1998 by
POETRY NOW
1-2 Wainman Road, Woodston,
Peterborough, PE2 7BU
Telephone (01733) 230746
Fax (01733) 230751

All Rights Reserved

Copyright Contributors 1998

HB ISBN 1 86188 724 8
SB ISBN 1 86188 729 9

FOREWORD

Although we are a nation of poetry writers we are accused of not reading poetry and not buying poetry books: after many years of listening to the incessant gripes of poetry publishers, I can only assume that the books they publish, in general, are books that most people do not want to read.

Poetry should not be obscure, introverted, and as cryptic as a crossword puzzle: it is the poet's duty to reach out and embrace the world.

The world owes the poet nothing and we should not be expected to dig and delve into a rambling discourse searching for some inner meaning.

The reason we write poetry (and almost all of us do) is because we want to communicate: an ideal; an idea; or a specific feeling. Poetry is as essential in communication, as a letter; a radio; a telephone, and the main criteria for selecting the poems in this anthology is very simple: they communicate.

Towards 2000 is a collection of poetry reflecting back on the last century and anticipating the next.

The poets in this anthology express their thoughts, feelings and emotions about their past; fond childhood memories, the way things used to be and how they have changed for the better or worse. While other poets await the year 2000, they view their expectations of the next century; better technology, world peace and even day trips to the moon!

Towards 2000 is an enjoyable poetry collection as it takes us on a journey through the past, present and future, showing some of the best poetry being written today.

CONTENTS

THE SPREAD OF AIDS

The spread of AIDS through having sex
May leave either partner feeling vex
AIDS destroys families and lives
And comes between husbands and wives.

The spread of AIDS is a serious thing
And only heartache will it bring
You need to use your common sense
Before your feelings become immense.

The spread of AIDS is not by chance
So now is the time to make a stance
Stop before you are too late
When you end up in a frenzied state.

The spread of AIDS during this decade
Is due to the sexual escapade
Sex needs to be viewed in a new light
Not just pleasure and pure delight.

The spread of AIDS is a growing trend
So we can no longer pretend
The way to stop the AIDS attack
Is by people no longer acting slack.

The spread of AIDS needs to be acknowledged
In the school, the university and the college
This is to ensure that AIDS is stopped
Before many more people are dropped.

Colin Hines

LESSONS, HOPES AND VESTIGES

In those early years of the 1900's man first mastered the
                                        secrets of flight,
Thanks to two brothers at Kittywake, named Wilbur and
                                        Orville Wright,
They took their heavier than air machine and flew, although at first
                                        not far,
But it paved a new frontier for mankind, that could point him to
                                        the furthest star.

The ruling and privilege class still ruled politics, with Liberals and
                                        Tories strong,
But a new socialist party for working people, Labour was born to
                                        a rousing song,
A time for new ideas and ideologies, a new sound with
                                        socialism's birth,
Suffragettes achieved votes for women-folk, thanks to the likes of
                                        Emmeline Pankhurst.

Horse-drawn carriages and far routed stagecoaches, would soon be
                                        a sight of our past.
Combustion petrol engine motor cars, were driven down new-made
                                        roads very fast,
A vibrating and rumbling beneath their feet, soon greeted Londoners
                                        with a new sound,
As electric motor driven tube trains, took new routes and destinations
                                        like moles underground.

Aspirin was discovered, manufactured and sold, for the relief of
                                        headaches and pain,
The tuberculosis germ was identified, lung disease would never be
                                        quite the same,
Great achievements like X-rays, penicillin, new discoveries in
                                        medicine, to name a few,
Medical advancements ground from long hours of research, promised
                                        cures for me and you.

During August 1914, the first great war was upon us, flags and bugles
blew grand,
While men of warring nations, fought to steal and protect
others' land.
After the sacrifice and heartache, with millions of deaths of children,
women and men,
We thought at last mankind had learned his lesson, alas 1939 saw
it all happen again.

The month of October 1957, saw the birth of the Space Age, Sputnik
and Yuri Gargarin led the way,
Followed closely by Alan Shepherd and John Glen, could the dawn
of a new era mark a much brighter day,
Neil Armstrong and Buzz Aldrin landed on our moon, that to earlier
man had seemed so far,
While Pioneer and Voyager spacecraft, left our solar system
journeying to another star.

Let us hope the 21st century, will be one of hope and co-operation
for all mankind,
If we overcome starvation, protect the environment, and all start
working together we may find,
That we could find our true place in the universe, a real intelligent
species at last,
And maybe we will benefit from all our yesteryears, and not repeat
those mistakes of our past.

Jim Wilson

To Name But A Few

The 20th century - the century of change
People left their mark right across the range
Many different reasons but all fondly remembered
As out of this century we step in 1999 - 31st of December

President Kennedy - Irving Berlin - Douglas Bader - Jack Ruby -
Karl Marx
Charlie Chaplin - Edward Elgar - Oscar Wilde - Amelia Earhart
Brian Epstein - Walt Disney - Roald Dahl - Marie Curie
Bobby Charlton - Laurel and Hardy - Alexander Fleming
Elvis Presley

Christopher Cockerell - Bob Dylan - James Bond - Thomas Edison
Lee Harvey Oswald - James Cagney - Clarence Birdseye - Richard
Branson
Agostini - Peter Sellers - James Hunt - Larry Adler - George Eastham
Diana Princess of Wales - Salvado Dali - Glenn Miller - Ian Botham

Bill Haley - Montgomery - Carl Lewis - Eusebio - Enid Blyton
Sean Connery - Beatrix Potter - Thomas Hardy - Richard Burton
Terry Waite - Henry Ford - Fred Perry - Pele - Sir Matt Busby
Eric Clapton
Donald Campbell - Castro - Benjamin Britten - Bobby Moore -
Richard Nixon

George Best - Dr Barnardo - Elizabeth Taylor - David Bowie -
Eric Bristow
Ron and Reggie Kray - Chubby Checker - Francis Chichester -
Brigitte Bardot
Tony Hancok - Alexander Graham Bell - Gary Sobers -
Nelson Mandella
Bob Geldof - Sir Alf Ramsay - Tommy Cooper - Roger Bannister

Louis Armstrong - Boris Becker - Berry Gordy - Yuri Gagarin
John Logie Baird - Adolf Hitler - Queen Victoria - George Gershwin
Sean Bean - Bob Marley - Jimi Hendrix - W G Grace - Albert Einstein
Winston Churchill - Martin Luther King - Yasser Arafat - James Dean

Julie Andrews - George Bush - John Lennon - Bonnie and Clyde
Woody Allen - Kingsley Amis - H G Wells - Sally Ryde
Fred Astaire - Ginger Rogers - Baden Powell - Neil Armstrong
Muhammad Ali - Gandhi - Mary Whitehouse and King Kong

All the people listed and we've only included a few
Left their mark on society in the world of who's who
Never has a century experienced change beyond recognition
As we move into the next century and see what has to come.

Leigh Smart

EYE ON THE PAST

An old tin bath, hung on outside wall
Any empty can, was our football
Conkers on string, the occasional fight
Old corner shop, where we gathered at night.
Fags cost a penny, smoke if you dare
Hand-me-down clothes, did anyone care?
Basin on head as your hair was cut
Gobstopper in mouth, to keep it shut.
Home-baked bread, rabbit stew in pot
Daren't leave table till you have eaten the lot
A birthday treat was to stay up late
An apple, orange, then watch fire in grate.
Roy Rogers, Gene Autrey, our heroes of course
Slap hands on hips, as we rode our horse.
Off to seaside in a rickety bus
Mam and dad making such a fuss
Then early to bed, for school next day
Nit nurse waiting to make her day.
Good times, bad times the dye was cast
But always there, is an eye on the past . . .

GIG

? . . . 42

People sitting on the roadside
While cars are choking up the street
Homeless lifted from the sidewalk
Pulled like rotten teeth

Houses standing empty
Children carry guns
Rain clouds made from factories
Rivers run with blood

The polar caps are melting
While there isn't any doubt
That the earth is slowly dying
As its skin is aged with drought

Its gift of life is wasted
And love is replaced by crime
Has man forgot the answer?
Has he now ran out of time?

We have questions left unanswered
To help us find the key
Before future generations
Blame its death on you and me

Mark Mawston

TIME LINE

From 1900 to 2000, a century of change,
From the 'Cakewalk' to the 'Twist' and to the 'Rave',
From when the Brits got their first taste of Coke,
To when London went up in smoke,
From Vera Lynn to Elvis Presley,
These were the days of the 20th century.

From Neil Armstrong, first man on the moon,
To the murder of John Lennon, the Beatle's tycoon,
But those golden days have now lost their grasp,
Technology has taken over (at last!)
Computers, cars and modems overrun,
The Third Millennium has just begun!

Haley Rose Cox (12)

SINGING NEVER STOPS

Return to this place the chorus of birds and colourful bloom
A congregation of survivors meet at the gates of doom.
Fifty years passed, but tears continue to shed
Searching for tombs that form a rose-bed.
A footstep taken through fear ridden nightmare
Each bead of sweat holds tales to compare.
The mind can play games for those idle folk
But true are these horrors which suck at their yolk.
Mother and father lay rest and now sleep
Yet time doesn't heal the wound from the weep.
Brothers and sisters, a life squeezed of breath
No-one could halt the Angel of Death.
Guinea pigs used and bodies to break
The cleansing of souls and ethnic forsake.
Thousands would sing in the showers of hell
Can deity save them from Hades' deep well.
An oven designed for Hansel and Gretel
Reality burned in these caverns of metal.
The soldiers of evil whose lives were a lie
Shall never find peace, tormented then die.
Museum of history with memories of sadness
But how can we stop dictators of madness.
Departing this place will tomorrow's children cope
These shrines of the sacred must bring us some hope.

Nicholas William James

A SIXTIES CHILD

I was a young Sixties child.
Just fifteen and rather wild.
Flower-power was out in full
Making our parents rather dull
Open air concerts, legs full of mud.
Oh! What a mess, but wasn't it good.
Mods and Rockers were in full swing
The Beatles and Monkees were the in-thing
Frothy coffee at the local caf!
Sipping it slowly and having a laugh.
Mini-skirts were all the rage.
It didn't really matter about your age.
Bright blue eyes, and lips of white
That seemed to glow in the disco light.
Mary Quant was really fab,
With psychedelic colours, it was never drab
The Swinging Sixties I remember it well.
There's so much happened and so much to tell.

Linda Woodhouse

THOSE 9 AND 7 YEARS

9 and 7 years have passed since you went away,
Those 9 and 7 years have passed as quick as yesterday.
Our little girls for us to keep and play with for all tomorrow's,
Robbed we are of your sunny faces, we only had to borrow.
When I think back to the days when we were all together,
There's such a gap now, never filled, to be with us forever.
The oddest things remind us of the things you'd say and do,
Like little signs to let us know it's just the both of you.
Although it seems hard without you, harder everyday,
Those 9 and 7 years have passed as quick as yesterday.

Catherine B Young

MOTHER TERESA

God put this lovely soul on earth,
To bring this whole world light,
She shone just like a shining star,
That makes the heavens bright,
She touched the hearts of millions,
And brought them love and peace,
She helped the homeless and the poor,
God's love she did release,
Poverty and bad disease,
Drug addicts and lots more,
Never did she judge one soul,
Her love on them, did pour,
God lived upon this earth, through her,
And taught her how to care,
If only we would take a leaf,
Out of her book so rare,
Then she would leave her truest gift,
In every human mind,
That love is such a wondrous power,
It can save all mankind,
So let us reach to others first,
And leave ourselves behind,
Then God will be our guiding light,
If we all seek and find,
So take my loving tribute,
To this very simple soul,
And a prayer, that she truly did,
Just reach her heavenly goal,
God Bless you for your human touch,
'Mother Teresa', you're loved so much.

Janette Campbell

THE CHANGING CENTURY

Of all the centuries that have been
With all the changes made,
This one has surely seen the most
The world has ever staged.
Man's cruelty in both thought and deed,
Of wars with such destruction
That could have blown mankind apart
No hope of reconstructions.

Technology beyond belief,
Rockets, and man in space,
Computers that are so advanced
Life moves at such a pace
We seem to have less time, not more,
Less tolerance, less thought,
Seeking materialistic gain,
With self-indulgence sought.

Women have won equality,
Independence and careers,
No longer men their masters
As in the distant years.
They take their place in Parliament,
Responsibilities share,
They've reached out over boundaries
Where once they wouldn't dare.

Battles won against diseases
While new ones start to thrive,
Hearts and lungs transplanted
To help us to survive.
This world, this life, so wonderful
Has changed throughout its days,
I'm glad I've lived to see it
In all its changing ways . . .

Vanda Gilbert

THE WORLD TODAY

Relaxing in front of the telly
Isn't like it used to be
Rapes, robberies and muggings
Are all you ever see
It gives me the shudders
When I watch our 'Northern Life'
Old people getting mugged
Or a husband's attacked his wife
What has gone wrong?
No-one seems to care any more
Can't walk the streets alone
Or even open your own front door
I know times are hard
And a lot haven't got a job
But beating up old people
Just for a couple of bob
It makes my blood boil
I sit, swear and curse
Especially when some old person
Tries to cling onto their purse
None of this would happen
If we had more bobbies on the beat
What I'd like to do to these people
I just dare not repeat
The law must get tougher
And then people just won't pinch
Because if it was up to me
I'd say 'Bring back the lynch.'

Eileen Glenn

DUNBLANE

Dark clouds of anger shrouding a mind
A mind no longer in tune,
Reality lost to the deafening roar
Of a dream fallen to ruin.

Try though he may to be recognised
There's no-one to hear his strange cry,
And someone must pay the price of his hate
Someone he'd destined to die.

On a grey morn as clouds hid the sun
He walked to the door of that school,
Deep in his thoughts there burned a desire
To break every God-given rule.

The little ones played beneath teacher's eye
Sweet innocence shining right through,
Then a cruel hail of death ended their fun
As he did what he had to do.

And angel from heaven descended on them
And paradise opened its door,
While in that bleak spot, silence did reign
And laughter could be heard no more.

Now they're lost forever and never again
Will their smiles light up each waking morn,
For gone is the joy once they did give
And the world can but feel forlorn.

Cherish the thoughts of those who have gone
But think of those who remain,
And may the sun ever shine brighter each day
On that brave little town of Dunblane.

Len Fox

TO THE WOMEN WHO DARED

They shortened their skirts
They cut their hair
They went unchaperoned everywhere.

They went out to work
They unashamedly smoked
They got their independence
And the right to vote.

To the rigids of Victorian life,
They were no longer confined.
They were expressing their own sexuality
And having a really good time.

No more waltzing in corsets,
Full skirts all a-twirl,
For these fully modern flapper girls.

Scantily clad,
Swinging their beads
Dancing to the Charleston
Flashing their knees.

But once they ventured,
Into the world of men
Life for women,
Was never the same again.

So as this century
Draws to a close,
Remember to whom the credit goes.

To all the women
Of the past who dared
To shorten their skirts
And cut their hair . . .

Who went unchaperoned everywhere.

Julie Ann Sloan

MILLENNIUM FOR WILLIAM

(Written early 1997 prior to Tom Finney's knighthood.)

Year two thousand is upon us
A whole millennium,
Presenting a whole hundred years
To our Prince William.

Millennium for William
What will he do with it,
Perhaps he'll knight Preston's Tom Finney
Who's done more than his bit.

What's in store for his two cousins
Beatrice and Eugenie,
Will they stay out of touch with public
And who will be his 'Queenie'.

At the closing of this chapter
The twentieth century,
Will conditions vastly change for the
Royalty and the gentry.

Hopefully he'll follow in his
Fond mother's goodly step,
And not ignore the sick and poor
But carry on, Britain's rep . . .

The greatest of greetings will be
When ninety-nine gets through,
A whole country says 'William,
Sir, - it's over to you.'

Barbara Sherlow

ENGLAND'S CENTURY

Looking back 100 years
Good times, bad times, laughter and tears
Memories of old still fresh in one's mind
Some best forgotten, best left behind.

World War One and World War Two
A place in history for me and you
But for those who were actually there
Hitler became their worst nightmare
Our lives today we thank them for
And pray the world will fight no more.

Fifties and Sixties saw Rock 'N' Roll,
World Cup triumph with that Geoff Hurst 'goal'
The Seventies became the 'glam rock' scene
With Bolan, Bowie, Glitter and Queen
The entire decade was such a delight
Platforms flares and colour so bright.

The Eighties arrived and the Tories were strong
With Maggie in charge they could do no wrong
The Falklands became a battleground
Our troops too strong, Argentina soon found
The Beatles now three, John Lennon shot dead
Charles and Diana soon to be wed.

The end of the Eighties saw Saddam Hussain
Giving Major no choice, it's war again
Now in the Nineties that we live in today
The year 2000 not far away.

A change of government now Labour are there
Led from the front by Tony Blair
And as the Millennium celebration starts
We remember Diana, our Princess of Hearts.

Kenny Page

OUR WORLD

Our world so full of speed and haste,
A world that ticks just like a time-bomb,
So much rubbish now is going to waste,

People so uptight and full of stress,
Always having too much to do,
No time to give and share their kindness,

So full of money, riches and greed,
Blinkered eyes are everywhere,
They do not see all those still in need,

Science and technology have leapt up to us fast,
All these things to make life easy for the rich,
Still leaving the poor and starving till the last,

Love and kindness and sometime to share,
A lot more giving to replace the taking,
Begin this world again with peace and care,

Take us to a new era of everlasting friendship,
A time to take care of our world before it's too late,
End this awful waste before too far the scales do tip.

Rebecca Simmonds

To Be Remembered

Since time began - *Many* - have left a name, to be remembered
They stand head and shoulders above, - the lesser breed,
Each *Century* has produced its crop of *Heroes* and *Villains*
Some - known for *Infamy* - and some for a famous deed.

The 20th *Century* is no exception
There was that *Frenchman,* flying over here - in a home-made plane
M Bleriot - who didn't give a hoot for *'air traffic lanes'*
And *Emily Pankhurst* and her *Suffragettes*
Who - in *London* - to railings tied their *Chains.*

In 1914 - the *Great War* was the battleground, for *Europe's*
young men
Until exhaustion forced *Germany* to the *Peace Table* - with
Lloyd George,
Whilst in *Russia*, after civil war - came communist leader *Lenin*
Who promised - a perfect workers paradise - to forge.

Later, came *Flyers* - *Amelia Earhart* - *Amy Johnson* and
Col Lindbergh
Those legends - with a fascination, for their *Flying Machines,*
And - jazz singer *Al Jolson* - with the new *Talking Pictures*
Beloved, - by the young - the middle-aged - and the in-betweens.

In the 30's, *Edward the 8th*, didn't relish the hard seat, of the throne
He preferred the soft arms of *Wallis Simpson* - an *American Divorcee*,
Whilst those *Big Bands,* - were soothing us - with dance music
From the likes of *Harry James* - *Arty Shaw* - and *Tommy Dorsey.*

Then came *Fire* and *Thunder* in the air, - over *Europe*
Hungry *Nazi Dictator, Adolf Hitler* - had a huge appetite,
But - with a little help from *Churchill* - *Roosevelt* - and *Stalin*
After 6 long years - he ate *Cyanide* for his *Last Bite.*

Now, in the *Post-War* world, - which - are the greatest names to
be remembered?
Would it be *Mohammed Ali? Margaret Thatcher?*
Or *Nelson Mandela?*
Maybe - *John F Kennedy? Pablo Piccaso? Luciano Pavarotti?*
Or - *Laurence Olivier?* footballer *Pele?* Or some other fella?

Paul Gold

REASONS FOR WHY

Upon the world I look
At a distance oh so far
Why man with all his wisdom
Will carry on and scar

So ruthless with his actions
And discussions that are made
Another tree will vanish
Another road is laid

Upon rich soil that once grew grass
And rabbits dear, had played
Now all dug, and levelled out
Not a hedge was saved

And what about the rivers
The ones that have run dry
Where have all the fish gone
I ask myself for why

Apart from that pollution
That fills the air we breathe
Also global warming
Not this I can't conceive

Now I look at all the nice things
That every day I see
And can't forget the past gone days
For how it used to be

Then I look at woodlands
And think it's well past time
Stop this cutting trees down
Especially in their prime

If we had a referendum
And we could make amends
Who needs these kind of enemies
When we could have these friends

E Tomlin

20TH CENTURY

Man has trodden on the moon and sent a probe to Mars and more,
Yet here on earth much of our land is covered with the scars of war,
And thousands die for lack of food and water
While others party, man and wife and daughter.

The greed of man is killing bears and tigers,
The filth of man pollutes our lakes and seas.
Our air and soil are full of noxious poisons
That are killing precious plants and trees.

We suffered two world wars and still there's fighting
And man kills man to gain a coin or two,
While others fight because their God is different
And evil reigns and good men they are few.

The assassin's bullet claimed two brothers who
Had rallied us to freedom's mighty call
And a King who spoke of equal rights,
Spreading the word of God to unite all.

How many more will die in years to come,
How many more will starve while others feast.
When will we learn to care and share
And know who has the most, has least.

Janette Anne Whiting

The Twentieth Century

The unsinkable Titanic
Sank in icy waters.
Fathers floundered with their sons,
Mothers with their daughters.
The course of history was changed
By Edward's abdication.
Wallis Simpson was blamed.
It really shocked the nation.
We've suffered wars and famine,
We've struggled through depressions.
When things did not improve
We blamed it on the recession.
What more can we achieve? We ask,
As the third Millennium looms.
We've discovered antibiotics,
And put men on the moon.
So what will the next century bring?
Will all the suffering cease?
For the sake of our children
Let us all pray for world peace.

Carol Liddle

MEMORIES

O bring back the sixties.
When Martin Luther had a dream,
and I could still do the twist.
Man stepped on the moon, and Kennedy was shot.
And I got by with a little help from my friends.

O give peace a chance.
We were told that we had not had it so good.
Those were the days my friends.
When a pound was worth a pound, and skirts were short.
And the mini and the Rolling Stones, said it all.

O those were the days.
When Ena Sharples sat in the snug,
and we all played Take-Your-Pick.
We all like to look back to happier times in our life
And I think to myself, what a wonderful world.

K A Davis

CHANCES . . .

I've been asleep, for, oh too, long awhile,
And now I'm wide awake.
I did notice that promise in your smile
But I faltered, and that is my mistake.

I've been asleep, for oh, too many days,
And now I'm trying to see
How many times, and how many ways
You tried to enamour me.

I should have been awake, I should have been there
To notice those lights of love in your eyes.
Been charmed by your grace; touched the shine in your hair.
I've been rash and foolish, not calm or wise.

I've been asleep, for oh, too many weeks,
And now I have to hope and pray
To find the elusive you, 'tis my quest to seek
As I get through yet another day.

I've been asleep, for oh, too many hours,
But now I'm wide awake again
I would love to say it with hearts and flowers.
Will I, can I, see you once more my beautiful friend?

Tony Heenan

UNTITLED

As the 20th century draws to a close
We have seen some extreme changes
The aeroplane was invented
Man flew as one, with the birds
He even went to the moon
We can talk to people all over the world
Thanks to the invention of the telephone
And now it's one step further
With the computer and all its wonders
We have so much to marvel at
In this ever-changing time
But there is also much to regret
Man has been careless about the environment
The wildlife needs so much care
If it is to survive, will we learn this lesson?
In time to ensure that there is a legacy
For future generations to enjoy
Medicine has made great advances
So many things that now can be cured
But still we sneeze when the dreaded cold strikes
So much has been achieved and so much has been learnt
But there is still a lot to do
And I guess it's up to all of us
To do our very best to bring this century
With all its joys and sorrows
To a peaceful end

E M Taylor

A PHILOSOPHICAL POINT OF VIEW

A new century dawns,
A regal lady mourned,
A new era was begun.
Extraordinary changes,
A world open wide,
A chance for us to learn.

Knowledge acquired,
And put to good use,
Was the hope of everyone.
Abuse of power,
Worldwide war,
Somehow it all went wrong.

Tyrannical oppressors,
Wielded power with verve,
History's lessons left unlearned.
Highly paid hypocrites,
Said no more of this,
How else can we keep them down.

So the bomb was swapped,
For capitalism,
A miserable existence.
This century,
A dynamic one,
To it, I say good - riddance.

The lessons we have learned,
I shall never know.
That's for you to scrutinise,
In the century to follow.
A regal lady mourned
A new millennium dawns.

Jayne Elizabeth Biggin

YEARS

The beginning of the century
Gave us the aeroplane
They flew it up, it came back down
They sent it up again

The First World War was next to list
Sending people to their graves
Everything was crashed and blitzed
Yet, nothing much was gained

The Charlton was the twenties
Gangsters and the rest
Smart men in suits, posh dressed
Women in stockings of mesh

Into the murky thirties
When miners dug for coal
Standing at the gates for work
Some signing on the dole

The forties saw another war
The biggest of them yet
Families carrying on with the sores
Remembering some they never met

Fifties and swinging sixties
The Beatles and The Rolling Stones
Mods and Rockers on their nifties
Now all that has gone

Seventies and Eighties progress
Videos, computers and games
The country was in a bit of a mess
But no-one ever mentions names

Nineties is getting so much nearer
To being a better planet
Everything is becoming clearer
To all the people left here on it.

Sammy Hagar

WAR

Years pass by, we should have learnt,
fighting never gets you anywhere
only the people suffer, watching as
their homes are burnt
the country they love laid bare.

And soldiers, throwing themselves
to the ground
faces covered all in mud,
bombs exploding all around,
land near, with an earth-shattering thud.

Mothers slowly going out of their minds,
not knowing if they have to mourn
their loved ones they've left far behind
children whom they once had borne.

So the politicians will argue
whilst others fight their wars
human lives they don't value
war makes them rich not poor.

Years pass by, another war rages on
in some other land
And time marches on.

Jeanette Snook

ARE SUCH MEN STILL OUT THERE?

Berliners sunbathing by city lakes
Women huddled trembling in a wood
Half-naked men bludgeoned to death by crowbar
Burying all human concerns beneath a larger goal

The smart floral dresses smile broadly
As the killers stand for their anthem
Unswerving dedication
Hand-crafted methods of liquidation

Not an inexplicable eruption of evil
But the marriage
Of bureaucratic determination and routine malice
Always ready for recruitment

Singular horrors
I know not
Singular people to commit them
I think not

How much did those sunbathers know?
Disappearance of common conscience beware
Such men
Are still out there.

B A Stone

UNTITLED

As you stand, staring up at me, a clipboard in your hand,
I wish I could tell you the things I've seen, to make you understand,

I've stood and watched a changing world for over a hundred years,
I've seen the peace, I've heard the wars and witnessed smiles and tears.

I protected small street urchins from wind and rain and cold,
And silently I watched as the young grew quickly old

Victorian men and their elegant ladies alight from carriages below,
Then enter the warm and plush new building that they would
                                                    frequent so

Then came the proud young men in uniform who marched on past
                                                    my windows
They smile at their wives and sweethearts who watch, but I'll see
                                                    the weeping widows

Now I see the world is changing as flowers cover the pavements below,
After two world wars and Vietnam, peace and love is the way to go

And so they smoke and play rock music, the young protest against
                                                    inhibition.
The stiff upper lip is castaway as they love one another without
                                                    condition

And so progression gallops on, they send a man up to the moon,
Noisy traffic escalates, pollution will be here soon

Now I am old, my windows smutty, foundations loose, my
                                                    brickwork grubby,
A homeless old man sits inside the door, I still give protection to
                                                    the poor

As new buildings tower above me, the man with the clipboard has
                                                    long gone away,
They have been built for the new Millennium, but I have had my day

Noisy machines slowly move forward, to gradually clear the site,
Once the grandest of them all, nobody hears my plight

The man looks on with a smile on his face, as he watches the
transformation take place
The work is done, the new century can come, I'll see it in with
Stately Grace!

Joy Beswetherick

CENTURY POEMS
(Dedicated to my mother Elizabeth Harriet Mercer, born Jan 7th 1895)

My mother Elizabeth will be
aged 103 on Jan 7th 1998
'God willing'
she has worked hard all her life
the eldest daughter in a family of nine
7 girls and 2 boys, her mother was married
at 16 yrs old and died aged 46 yrs.
We were evacuated to Cornwall at
the start of the war and have lived here ever since,
she helped everyone, working right till she was in
her nineties
to assist us in our business,
and took a great interest in young people,
she is loved by so many people.
Reaping the love she has given
over so many years.

Pauline Elizabeth Morris

CLONING GRACE

When Andy Warhol took the beans
And mass-produced the image,
The thought of cloning human beings
Was just a passing whim.
But now a sheep called Dolly
Has changed the vision for us.
Instead of mass-producing slides, you see,
We can mass-produce our Grace.
        One, two, three, fours,
        Let's clone some more.

Doreen King

OUT OF WORK

I used to rise at six each day
Take breakfast then to work, on my way
Then from my boss, the dreaded letter
I'm afraid your finished work gets no better.

Now I sit here in my chair
I really am in despair
Jobs vacant I read in papers each night
For every application I put up a fight.

No cigarettes or beer for me
I really need things that are free
My dole I draw each second week
It's a job that I must really seek.

Now as the days and months go by
I'm sitting here and wondering why
There is no offer of a job
I feel that I am just a slob.

I'm not afraid to work all day
For just the chance I often pray
At one time I had a wife
She became depressed and took her life.

Now that I am left alone
No wife, no pets, no telephone
I have no shoulder upon to cry
But for that job I shall still try.

Ray Jacks

POEMS FOR A CENTURY - PROGRESS?

I can remember fondly when cars were rare and new,
And aeroplanes were luxuries for the rich and favoured few.
The pace of life was slower, hi-tec, a thing unknown,
All was safe unguarded and one could walk alone.

All this has changed as years went by,
Aircraft got bigger, it's quicker to fly.
Cars are a must, so more roads were built,
And now cross the country, like a patchwork quilt.

Quickly the space-age came on the scene,
Probing the heights where no man had been.
Their target, the yellow far away moon,
Man, they said would walk on it soon.

With all this accomplished what else have we got,
The masters of science now want to play God.
Can this be called progress where will it all end,
As nature and all of the rules they bend.

As the next era looms, we can be sure of one thing,
God goes before and knows all it will bring.
We need to be watchful, we toil not in vain,
For His promise is sure 'I will come again.'

F L Brain

WHO IS GREAT GRANDMA?
(For the women of two World Wars)

'Great Grandma would have approved,'
How often we read these words
applied to some resurrected custom,
or mock modest mode of dress.

But who is this mythological lady?
If the writer of the article
is middle-aged, or rather less,
then Great Gran is certainly not
the full-skirted, fragile girl
who blushingly drank afternoon tea
with a young gentleman
to the tinkle of silver spoons
against fine china.

More likely she is a woman
who spent her girlhood
wearing khaki trousers,
battling against the Hun
alongside the men,
as ghostly searchlights lit skies
thick with death, or perhaps she drove
ambulances in streets of blazing danger,
perhaps she nursed the incredibly wounded,
or shovelled vegetables,
in mudded fields of necessity . . .

or waited for her man,
surrounded by his children
in a flimsy shelter
propped up by the courage
of her singing . . .

so please don't patronise,
for neither Gran, nor Great Gran,
in younger days, striding vigorously,
through life's vicissitudes
ever resembled the frail wraith
of your untutored imagination.

M Munro Gibson

20TH CENTURY

From horse and cart
Golly, where to start?
Mr Ford's mobile cars
and travels to the stars.
Radio to television,
to space exploration.
Things called stivengraphs,
and people put in photographs.
Mrs Simpson got a divorce,
jokes about Edward, very coarse.
Few are the liners on the seas,
fewer too, the forests of trees.
Aeroplanes crowd our skies,
as our planet slowly dies.
Yet all this is called progress;
but the 20th
century is some mess!

Ursula Meldon

THE 21ST CENTURY

The 21st century
What will it bring?
More poverty, war
And even more famine.
What can we do,
To stop this and bring
No more poverty, war
And no more famine?

Tiffany Aubrey (13)

THE 2ND MILLENNIUM - A DISASTER?

One thousand years, for humans, is the blinking of an eye
From dinosaurs, and cavemen, to rockets in the sky
Technology, a modern world, one giant step for mankind,
From quill-pens, to fountain pens, and guide dogs for the blind
Two world wars, killing scores, thousands maimed and dying
Peace at home, but not abroad, some tyrant always trying.
Longbows gone, flintlocks too, chain guns and lasers now.
We haven't learnt a damn thing still, the arsenal grows and grows,
And so do lines of refugees, of every creed and kind
Ethnic cleansing, genocide, dictators, whole countries mined.
Communications beyond belief, radio, TV, mobile phone
Hello to friends, from car or plane, from satellites on their own
'Hello earth, we've landed, we're standing on the moon.'
'We'll collect some grey rock samples, be home Friday afternoon.'
Word by phone, by telefax, they've sent a drawing through
We can see the man in France, we are actually talking to.
Musically the scene has moved from cylinders to CD's
Vinyl out, stereo in, the sound is the 'bees knees'
From classical to rock and roll, jungle, techno, rap and soul
From Woodstock to all night raves, where 'Ecstasy' takes it toll.
Multi-cultural countries, bring colours and creeds together
The world zest for life, and change, no-one can ever tether.
Sexual equality, lesbians, gays, the closet doors are gone
Moral standards lowered, bondage, AIDS, the list goes on and on.
Cleaner seas, pollution curbed, the earth has had a summit
Forest gone, fish-stocks down, looks like we'll have to slum it
Human transplants, hearts and lungs, artificial tickers.
Long queues in the NHS, but none for private pickers
New source of power, the nuclear age, bombs and power stations
Let's hope the third Millennium brings peace to all earth's nations.

B M Hurll

ELEGANT IN ALL ITS GLORY

Elegant in all its glory,
This county narrates its own story.
From cobbles and miners, wool and writers,
This county has produced its own historical fighters.
A county lived through numerous ages,
And has covered countless pages.

Brontë and Hughes are names which may confuse,
Poets and writers become bemused,
From the changes and contrasts of town and city,
Of village, field, fell, dale, stream and valley.
Let this be a lesson to be learned,
For things to stay the same, they have to be earned.

Yorkshire and cricket unite as one,
Aims of victory are just a mere sum.
Something to be noted for proffers an honourable and
humble feeling,
Waiting for the time when success becomes apparent as
a seedling.
Lord behold, life of this county has not yet begun,
There is much, much more to chance upon.

Hence respect this county through generations,
Age and growth result in mere alterations.
However the character of the county remains the same,
And visitors go away feeling glad that they came.
May it always remain this way,
And be a valuable source for the jay.

Elana Henderson

FOUR - LANE LANE

Trains and boats and planes
Whisk you to faraway places
Without trace
Faster even than the speed of sound.
Come fly with me,
Come die with me,
Should you survive the holocaust
Then cry for me.

Cry for me a river
Tears to swell an ocean,
Then sail into the sunset on a never-ending cruise
And lose yourself
In sorrow and devotion,
Yet should the morrow, you survive the sinking of the cargo
Still cry for me.

Returning hence from where you came
Via American Express
Or any fast train, to carnage in suburbia
Travel first-class
Accept nothing less,
Then should you still survive disintegration
Cry for me, still cry for me.

Through tears, fire then your faithful mustang, haste
To frenzy in a four lane lane
Of flesh and metal, tears and pain,
And waste no more
Your optics
To cry for me
Come, fly with me,
Come die for me.

Susan Colyner

THOUGHTS OF CENTURY

Street lamps lit where children use to play,
War and Peace
Soldiers, children, people,
great leaders gone! To their
rest, memory of music and songs,
still remain with us,
Marilyn Monroe, spoke in sweet voice,
Teddy Boys came in went out with rock and roll
Elvis sang well, Beatles top of pops.
Assassination of president,
man walked on moon.
Invention, technology gave new lift to life
fashions went out
in came the new.

Kathleen Keating

VE DAY

Victory in Europe was fifty years ago today.
Everybody wanted to celebrate on that day in May.
They also remembered those who did not come home.
Never more to see their families, never more to roam.
Some of us only know by heroic tales told.
About every service man or woman, all daring and bold.
They all did their duties without making a fuss.
Fathers and mothers saying we all had medals given to us.
We are all proud to sing, 'Land of Hope and Glory'.
And hopefully still find time to listen to every story.
Every child should be taught to cherish this date.
Fifty years on, a fitting reason to celebrate.

Elizabeth Ann Allingham

CENTURY PAST

The wonders of the engine
Electricity gas and steam
Computers, radio and atom
Inventors more than dream
An end to polio and smallpox
Antibiotics against many ills
An army of liberated ladies
Babies stopped, by taking pills
Weapons far more deadly
Than any known to men.
Rockets in space, man on moon
Progress please think again
A world where children go hungry
A land not safe to play
Because of landmines left behind
When the soldiers went away
A world not tolerant of difference
Be it gender, colour or creed
Forests burnt, animals extinct
In the name of progress or greed
To the children of the new Millennium
Inherit your world with a sigh
Forget power and glory, let love rule your world
Make a new start at least you can try
Be at one with all around you
Heal the world for everyone's sake
But most of all our children
Please learn from our mistakes.

Dianne Roberts

THE SENSELESS WAR

In a field of blood in some faraway place
A young man lies dying with tears on his face
In the background, the guns play a war requiem
Each bullet that's fired is quick to condemn
He tries to make sense of man killing man
But he knows that the answer is, nobody can
He prays that his death will not be in vain
That a lesson is learned and no more are slain
Then he pictures his mother, alone and in tears
And hopes that her grief will ease with the years
There's sadness at leaving with words unspoken
But knows his memory will live on in the hearts
that are broken
And now there's a silence, here comes the angels
who weep
I'll just close my eyes now and go to sleep.

S Powell

UNTITLED

A new sign of the times, I hear you say
Well do you remember that fateful day,
In loving memory of Dunblane
Who lost their lives was so insane
A ban on hand-guns, people did cry
Now, watch the complaints come flying by,
So what about the guns on the street
The ones the deadline doesn't meet
These are the ones we have to stop
The guns police need to get on top,
Banning all guns isn't the answer,
Get the guns that lead song and dancer.

Dee Rhys-Jones

ONWARDS WE TRAVEL

Upon this highest mountain
I turn my face unto the sky
Feeling the kiss of Jesus
As I slowly close my eyes

How humble I feel upon this mountain
Where so many have trod before
All but reaching to heaven
To knock upon God's door

Onward we travel northward
Revelling beauty so rare
High to the home of the north wind
Where once wild cats had their lairs

Becoming a part of history
With those who have stood here in awe
On foot or horseback they travelled
Over road mountains and moors

I believe I can hear their laughter
As tall grasses dance in the breeze
Or is it their prayers they are whispering
Perhaps young loves, as sweetly they tease

Year upon year, people cometh
Footsteps now lost in the dust
Joining souls for infinity
For I know this to be true and just

Weaving a web like a spider
Silver circles without beginning or end
Hands to touch hands never stopping
Life's circle continues my friends

Susan Goldsmith

THE TWENTIETH CENTURY

The twentieth century is one
Historians will never forget
Two world wars and the dropping
Of two atom bombs
Are incidents we all regret

The sudden death of John F Kennedy
Princess Grace, Elvis and Princess Diana
Dramatised us one and all
The events of Lockerbie and Dunblane
Are two others I recall

There were also many inventions
Over the last hundred years
Which has made life more durable
As we all journey through
This valley of tears

The electric bulb, radio
Moving pictures and TV
The electric Hoover, fridge
Washing machine and telephone
I do hope you agree

The conquering of Mount Everest
And man walking on the moon
The advances in medicine
And communications
Are all set to boom

Edward Biggins

THE PRESIDENT'S LAST DAY IN OFFICE

The scene is set in Dallas
it's November 22nd 1963
a date never to be forgotten
by a world, a nation or family.
The president is being driven by,
waving to the cheers
his supporter's faces are all smiles
but shortly they'll be covered by tears.
The troubles he has faced
with Cuba, Russia and war
are clearly far from his mind
as he has a worse fate in store.
As the open-car turns the corner
he continues to wave with his wife
the Lincoln passes the book depository
where the assassin aims to take his life.
A shot rings out from above
striking him in the head
he lays cradled by his wife
her pink suit now stained blood red.
As the president's life leaves him
the assassin is quickly sought
in an all-day showing cinema
was where Oswald was caught.
He continually voices his innocence
scapegoat for a conspiracy
even when he too is murdered
no-one hears his plea.

The greatest puzzle of the century
did Oswald kill the president or a conspiracy.

Dale Short

RWANDA

In the sap of time daybreak falls
faceless like the wind
a wheel slowly turning
like a peeling orange
No smell of the lime clothes
In the sun colour
As light intercepts the darkness
Within the eyes
All the pain came from the rhyme
That bezoo the stench of death
While knuckles tissues dresses
The tears to the tune of tiny drums
Played by a thousand crying tongues
The lyrics a cry for help to the rest of the world
Who stood by and watch
The genocide and atrocities been
Committed against Rwanda people.

Prince Marley

THE ISLAND PRINCESS

Resting from life's troubles,
Diana - our English rose
Garlanded with flowers
At peace
Final repose
In her familial island
Of childhood days
Never to be forgotten
With our love she stays.

Tamar Segal

ONWARD WE MUST GO

What do we look for at the turn of the century!
Hope, for a better future, peace and goodwill
Those who were there, saw a future queen born
although they and she knew it not.
But a few years rolled by, then came the war,
Where had the peace gone, which we all prayed for
Mothers' lost sons, wife lost husband,
Four years of sadness and tears, all over the land,
Then peace at last, but only for a few short years
Twenty years was not long to build a new life
Again we had war, much worse than before
But once again, sweat, tears, and blood were shed
No-one was safe at their work, or in their bed
Children were sent abroad to lands far away
Some never came back, they preferred to stay
Never to see their loved ones again
At long last, peace, once again was declared
From pain and sorrow, no-one was spared
We now have a new queen on the throne
Forty five years have since passed along
That same queen is still on the throne
We also have strife amongst ourselves
We often wish for things that might have been
How can we hope for peace in the world
When we still have greed and jealousy prevailing
What we can do and should do, is hope and pray
For a much better outlook, to take us into the next century,
We can never turn the clock back so go forward,
Into the next century, and make a better world, for everyone.

Olive Wright

FORWARD TO TOMORROW

In 1901 Queen Victoria died
then all of Britain mourned
and like a child much heralded
the century was born

Our fickle Earth
so full of hope
knew not what was in store
by 1914 Britain and the world had gone to war

The forties brought the holocaust
to Europe's bloody shores
Pray God we learnt our lesson
in the horrors of both wars

Post war years brought harmony
We'd seldom known before
and by 1957 we were clamouring for more

The Comets 'rocked around the clock'
Petula sang 'Downtown'
and fathers throughout all the land
yelled 'Turn that music down'

By the Sixties and the Seventies
we'd really come to life
and the Dallas assassination
had bereaved a loving wife

The century now at an end
brought laugher, fears and sorrow
and citizens of all the world
look forward to tomorrow.

John Charlesworth

RECOLLECTIONS OF A CENTURY

We can look to the new Millennium with pride in our nations,
The inventions of the last century have given us pleasures and
Relaxations.
We have so much that makes living so easy.
It's hard to believe our forefathers lives were so measly.
No life support machines and transplants to keep them alive.
Just primitive medicine to help them survive.
Emergency services weren't so quick off the mark,
And were usually pulled by horse and cart.
No tractors or harvesters to help sow and reap,
It was very hard work without much sleep.
Cooking, washing and cleaning were quite a toil,
Even the kettle took hours to boil.
Our food wouldn't last long, now, without fridge or freezer.
They couldn't go for a take-away burger or pizza.
What pleasures did they have when round a log fire they sat,
Without television and radio or a telephone to chat.
What would they think of the motorways, congested with cars.
There wasn't buses, trains or even rockets to the stars.
I doubt if they would believe we've had men on the moon.
Satellite TV and computers, that are a boon.
To schools and the work place and surfing the Net,
We can go round the world in liner or jet.
Look at videos and photographs of places not to forget.
Looking back on the centuries without those products of genius.
It makes me wonder if we've had it all to commodious.
This wonderful world full of creations by man.
Means we can look to the next millennium as we plan,
Worldwide celebrations of festivities with glee
That will go down in history as the greatest we will ever see.

Patricia Taylor

ELVIS PRESLEY

'Heartbreak Hotel', in nineteen fifty-six
was Elvis Presley's very first hit.
Soon after his songs were being played worldwide
by this guy so handsome and full of pride.

He sang the gospel, but mostly rock
most of his records went straight to the top.
Acting became another part in his life,
soon he met Priscilla and made her his wife.

He took her to his mansion which was named Graceland,
they walked through the door together holding hands.
Soon a daughter was born to this happy pair
gorgeous she was and so very fair.

Suddenly Priscilla and Elvis went their own way
what happened between them I cannot say.
From then on Elvis was never the same
upon himself he took all the blame

Eventually this man, the 'King of Hearts'
at too young an age, did depart
From this world to a place above the sky
but here on earth his memory will never die.

Irene Joan Blair

FOR OUR TODAY

In a far off field where poppies sway
Beside an unknown grave
A mother bows in honoured prayer
Remembering the brave.

Silent her sorrowed tears befall
To kiss the time etched stone
Deep in her heart a yearning still
He could have been her own.

With dignity the silence *seals*
The pledge mankind must keep
To honour those in unknown graves
Where now the poppies weep.

Malcolm Wilson Bucknall

IN THIS CENTURY

In this century
What has really happened?
Who really knows?
Trying to talk to old grandad
'When I was in the war.'
He goes just like
Old Albert from Only Fools and Horses
Trying to talk to mum and dad
'In my day we could go out with a pound note, today forget it.'
I get told
Who really knows what happened
Over this last century
Wars
Yeah
New inventions
Of course
New designs
No not really
New coins
Yeah
New Government
Yeah
I get told
In this century

Mel Leggett

A Very Special Era

The twentieth century was a unique time
A very special era
Knowledge expansion of mankind
As the space age draws so nearer

A picture box of acts and shows
That soon become religion
This gift which had no colour
Became known as television

Elvis struts his stuff on stage
While performing in a show
Male hearts thump at their dream date
Miss Marilyn Monroe

Tragedy spreads far and wide
To the death of JFK
In two world wars so many died
Bombs from the IRA

Prouder times have happened too
Neil Armstrong stands so tall
East and west found compromise
At the fall of the Berlin Wall

Inventions came in different ways
PC's, the Atom Bomb
CFC brought UV rays
The poison from our sun

The twenty first is vast approaching
Do we have just what it takes?
To live in peace around the world
And learn from our mistakes.

Jason J Rorbach

MOMENTOUS TIMES

Our twentieth century
has seen the dawning of the space age -
nuclear power with atomic energy -
the birth of radio - talking pictures -
television and computer technology.

We've boasted
a new Elizabethan Age in a Festival of Britain
after two world wars - free from tyranny -
Mount Everest was conquered by a British Expedition
Hillary and Tensing reached the summit on Coronation Day '53.

Via television
we've seen Neil Armstrong first footing on the Moon -
we recovered from the shock of The Great Train Robbery -
we saw the rise and fall of Prime Minister Margaret Thatcher -
celebrated Elizabeth II Silver Jubilee.

We experienced
a wind of change with Premier McMillan -
world travel became a breeze flying with Concorde supersonically -
we survived industrial strikes - Beatlemania and decimalisation -
Royal Weddings - divorces and heart-rending tragedy.

A new millennium is now fast approaching
we're looking forward to bidding hello -
its been fun winging down the ages
into the 21st Century - here we go.

Lucy Green

THOUGHTS

Events of the past one hundred years
some with hope, some with fears.
Heroes battled in two world wars
fighting for their countries cause.
With nuclear bombs now invented
on Nagasaki and Hiroshima they were tested.
The destruction witnessed by these disasters
made the arms race grow even faster.
Then man built a rocket and flew into space
took his first steps on the moon's face.
Pictures of earth were beamed back to us
showing our planet so precious.
The cold war began to cease
could this be the start of world peace?
People tore down the Berlin Wall
giving hope to one and all.
But as the third millennium nears
we now have new fears.
AIDS, the Ozone and Global Warming
for mankind's future to survive, we must heed nature's warning.

Rhoda Jacobs

DUNBLANE

A news flash in the morning
left the nation stunned
People questioned God and faith
Why do the good die young?

The killer, a lone gunman
his motive is unknown.
Could there ever be a reason
for such a heinous crime.

Reports show frantic parents,
emotions fill their minds.
Relief, then guilt and sorrow
as they take their children home.

Bobbie Hurdman

THE TITANIC DISASTER 15TH APRIL 1912

They marvelled at her Majesty - the likes we've never seen,
Her size, her looks, her magnitude - a liner beyond dream.
It was her 'Maiden Voyage', her decor very fine,
Her staircase and her dining room, her chandeliers divine,
With pride she carried passengers, 1500 (hundred) but a few,
The young, the old, the rich, the poor - a life to start anew!
She sailed away upon the brine -
The flagship of 'The White Star Line'.
Into the night with all on board -
With engines 'full' the liner roared,
The passengers now unaware of what would lie ahead
They thought she was 'unsinkable' or that was what was said.
The telegraph gave warnings - the danger was made clear
But still the Captain told the crew the course they had to steer,
The men up in the 'Crow's Nest' realised their plight,
The iceberg loomed in front of them - it was an awesome sight.
'Slow to the starboard bow - be careful as we go,'
But beneath the freezing waters the iceberg lay below.
'To the decks, man the lifeboats' - alas the Captain said,
But in 2 hours - forty minutes she lay on the ocean bed.
Some lives were saved - hundreds lost,
No-one in Maritime History could ever count the cost.
Below the Atlantic Ocean will be their resting place
An unexpected tragedy of the human race.

Maureen Thomson

POPPIES THROUGH A CENTURY

O'er French fields where poppies bloom,
The brave in rows are lying
There is silence and in gloom
Red heads waft in a breeze crying
For it's there they lie for eternity
As our life goes on each day
Fears of history enshrined finally
Through dawns and sunsets always
As hearts cry out, tears roll down
The memories of loved ones gone
For sacrifice they're renowned
Red poppies still bloom at dawn
With all the love and prayers
We could not have them back
A final curtain was theirs
All dreams for the future they lacked
So as they sleep amongst the poppies
With the winds blowing o'er
We will remember it was for us
They reached their golden shore

Janet L Murray

FORTY YEARS

For forty years you have been our Queen
So many changes you have seen
Two wars been fought and many died
The Queen and Country by their side
With Prince Philip there with pride
Has been a father and a guide
Now your subjects warm and true
Send many blessings now to you.

J Willson

A WEATHER WARNING

El Nino is coming
We've had them before,
But nature so powerful
Has declared war.
In past years she's warned us,
A mother like hen,
But now she feels threatened
By arrogant men,
Whose first love is money
They care not to give
Much thought to conserving
The world where we live.

So batten the hatches
Fasten the main,
We've gambled with nature
We've made her insane,
She's angry and pulsing
Hysterically mad,
Unleashing her wild side
All stormy and sad.
The seas hot and steaming
Rise up in great clouds,
She viciously blows them
To panic the crowds!

A 20th Century
Nightmarish scene,
Let's calm Mother Nature
For she is the Queen.

Irene Carter

THIS SECOND MILLENNIUM

T wo thousand years,
H ow time has flown by!
I s this world a better place,
S ince in His innocence, Christ they did crucify?

S aviour of a world destined to die;
E verywhere, victims of war, hunger, homelessness, despair.
C ry Oh! Why God, why? On silent ear.
O n Your Son's beautitudes, we learn too late to impart.
N ow God gave all men, this earth to share.
D oes race, colour, creed matter? It's the heart, the soul, my dear.

M ust we judge others by the former, when the latter is the key,
I s not loving each other, the holding hands together,
L iberating the insanity of war and hate?
L ove is all we need, don't make heavy weather,
E ven if life is difficult, we must pull together, united.
N otional, this is no imaginary dream of humble me!
N o beings with hunger, homelessness, violence blighted.
I mpossible!' I hear you cry 'Such a world we'll never see.'
'U nited in peace and harmony.'
M ight we just try? It begins with you. It begins with I!

Peter William Percival Turner

A BRIGHT NEW YEAR

Looking back we now reflect,
The wars, the triumphs, the lives, the deaths.
Heroes, villains, saints and sinners
Without which we'd have no past.

The world has gone through many changes,
Some from decline to a happier status.
Some from good to bad to worse,
But no change could make earth perfect.

But through the 16 years of my life,
I have to say, I've had a good time.
The 80's were a lot of fun,
Growing up in this wondrous world.

And now I look forward to an exciting new start,
As the 3rd Millennium dawns upon us,
Saying goodbye to the 20th Century,
Welcoming in a bright new year.

Roxanne Drake (16)

Tin Mines

Our era now is dying,
Where stacks and chimneys stand
Pointing like fingers to the skies,
The cage wheels stark and still,
Silent and rusting,
Around the wild moorland
The west wind coldly sighing.

From tin mine to tin mine,
From Geevor to Levant,
In the valleys and on hilltops,
Where stopers and drillers
Went down on evening core,
Where miners broke new ground
Along the western shore.

From Pendeen to Morvah
And from St Just to Zennor,
From Redruth and Camborne,
In the misty evening shadows
Come echoes ringing
In the long hours of lonely nights
Of miners' voices singing.

Esme Francis

POEM FOR A CENTURY

What happened to the world we knew
What happened to our pride
Instead of front doors open now
We hide behind them inside
There's no love and understanding
Let's try to help each other
Why should we have to destroy
This life for one another
It needs us all to turn around
And open up all our hearts
Make the next century work for us
Don't tear it all apart.
We only have one chance you know
Let's make this the one
The century to make it
Life could be so much fun

Janet Dronsfield

MEMORIES OF FRIENDS AND SHIPS

My working life, I played my part,
With fellow workers, in a local shipyard.
We *fashioned ships,* from wood and steel.
Working in wind, sun and snow.
Together we made those ships grow.
How proud we were on those days,
To see those ships as they were floated away.
Factories and buildings now occupy *that* sight,
Where we toiled, day and night.
Those *shipyards* have now long gone,
But memories and friendships forever live on . . .

Brian Marshall

VE DAY (MAY 1995) BATTLE FOR FREEDOM - A THOUGHT FOR THE BRAVE (1939-45)

Those brave young men of years gone by
Who fought on land, on sea or sky
Why did they die?

Did they know this Land of Ours
Would turn into a wreath of flowers,
Our youth today a bunch of cowards
Who while away their makeshift hours
Why did they die?

Perhaps they were the lucky ones
Who fought for peace with bombs and guns,
They gave their lives without a thought
As long as Freedom dear was brought
To the land they loved beyond compare
England - the land of love so rare.
But the grandchildren for whom they died
Have no ideals or sense of pride.
Why did they die?

The spirits of those brave young men
Are in a place of peace again.
God knows they fought with hearts of love,
But tears now flow from up above.
They did not live to see this land
Be torn apart by youth's own hand
And see the state their country's in
For which they gave up everything.

That's why they died.

Jill Silverman

THE TWENTIETH CENTURY

Started in the year of our Lord, nineteen hundred AD
What wonders and advancement did we see
Over the last one hundred years so much has happened
Like a piece of cloth well marked and patterned
But how many died in the terrible disasters
How many men thought they could be the world's master
1914 to 1918 the first world war
Oh how high the casualty numbers did soar
What a waste of four good years
Four hard years of sorrow and tears
Then after the war all the sorrow and pain
Good men going over to fight in Spain
Good men from Jarrow marching to London, demanding
A decent wage a job a house a decent landing
Twenty years on, another war
Greedy Hitler demanding more
The Holocaust that never happened all propaganda
While Hitler sat high in his mountain retreat viewing the world from
That veranda
The war in Korea, should we have been there
The angel of Dien Bien Fu, Oh we all said a prayer
Then into Vietnam the mistake of the century
Most of those sent there ended their days in penury
All the mistakes that were made, mostly untold
Did we progress so far when there's no cure for a cold
No cure for cancer the world riddled with AIDS
Only three years to go before this century fades
Oh God hear my plea on this cold winter's day
Take us into the next millennium without delay.

June Clare

PAST PRESENT AND FUTURE

I've been thinking back to the last century,
And about the people who were then alive,
I've been wondering if they were still with us,
Would they view our world with pride?

The virtues that those folk lived by,
And held in such high esteem,
Would appear to have almost vanished,
And vice now reigns supreme.

We speak little today of integrity,
Good-example, honesty, or trust,
Modesty, respect or loyalty,
But to them these things were a must.

Our conversation now is of other things,
Like violence, greed and crime,
Murder, robbery, sex and drugs,
Which are so rife in our time.

This century has brought many changes,
And wonderful things have been done,
But can we please bring back some virtues,
So that evil may be overcome.

As we welcome the new millennium,
Let us embrace everything that is good,
May all of our people be happy,
And enjoy life as they should.

Mary Brady

WHERE DOES MAN GO?

Where does man go, now that the vastness of life
has shrunk to laptop computers and television?
As the millennium looms it seems that man has not
learnt his lesson, nor as the 20th century dies,
has he maintained his ability to see or feel.
Where are the men who booted the world into
the industrial age, those defenders of new ideas?
Where are the men who put paint to canvas,
inspiring the world around them with colour?
Where are the men, both deaf and blind, who
soared to another plane with the power of their
music, and took us with them to a new world?

People like Dickens and Austen left behind them
a vast store of thought that gripped our hearts and
souls, but with them died the ability to inspire
each other by word or to hear the other man speak.
Politicians such as Gladstone and Lloyd George
set their mark in social reform, and yet we hear
only an echo of their work in our small mean world.
We are consumed by technology and science,
we have seen the world's faith die at the hands
of the Internet and the selfishness of mankind.
Where does the heart and soul of the 1990's sleep,
barren with futile politics that mouth empty words?

As the year 2000 looms, mankind has to learn to listen,
he has to seek the truth again that lies beyond the PC.
Amongst our mediocre buildings, and bickering politics,
there may still be an essence of true meaning of life,
and that somehow greatness still exists in the soul of man,
if we but look with our hearts and not our eyes.

Jacki Larcombe

POEM FOR A CENTURY

The years we have, seem to fly so fast
Through people, places, times and events
But every moment from what people have had
It's something special that everything meant.

People have had a few good times
Some of us have had a few bad days
From the years behind, we kept all the thoughts
But it's a shame most thoughts always fade.

It wasn't long ago, since our parents were kids
Now look at us, we're their young ones
They have brought us up so good and bright
And took good care of us through day and night.

Some of us young ones
Grow wise beyond our years
Taking the short time, to grow up to fast
Letting our childhood, move quick to the past.

They say today, that 'Life's too short'.
Some of us don't even give life a go
Some of us move on from what we've been taught
To of chosen a good future and let our life grow.

The future years are coming ahead
It has flown that fast to have come so quick
Weeks, months and years have speeded its way behind
All the time has disappeared like a magic trick.

Now we have to look forward
To what we'll have and keep it together
To get all what we want out of life
As we will not be here forever.

Natalie Hill

A CENTURY CONDENSED

I count myself lucky I've seen a large part
Of a century with so many things
The great ship Titanic and two World Wars
Edmund Hillary and Sherpa Tensing
Emily Pankhurst and JFK
Winston Churchill, now he was a boon
Monty and Ike and Luther King
Oh yes and a man on the moon
Edward the 7th, he gave up his throne
To be with the woman he loved
Our precious Diana, the Queen of our Hearts
Was re-claimed by the angels above.
Silent movies and radio too
Chaplin and Morecombe and Wise
Talkies, TV and the telephone
We couldn't believe our eyes
Land speed records, great moments in sport
Jesse Owens, Seb Coe, Sally Gunnell.
The jet plane and Concorde flying at speed
And trains through the new Channel Tunnel
Bill Haley came in with his rock 'n' roll
Sinatra and Elvis - 'The King'
Along came The Beatles with their 'Yeah Yeah Yeah'!
In contrast to crooners like Bing
Washers that wash and dryers that dry - keyboards that play
by themselves
All of these things you can buy in a store, all stacked up high
on their shelves

Computers and printers and digital 'things'
Technology's now all the rage
There's no doubt about it, I'm really quiet sure
I've lived in a wonderful age.

Gwen Harper

PROMISE

Our century is closing, it's drawing to an end
But sometime in the middle
We promised a man
We would send
One summer day in sixty nine
Three men travelled
For the very first time
An image flickered in black and white
Perhaps this time
We had got it right
While one man waited
And flew up above
And eagle had landed
But not a dove
Footprints that would last
For an age
Were that very day
On every front page
Time it was passing
And air would run low
And so from Selen's face
Our men had to go
No last backward glances
Nor shouts of farewell
Just back to the mother
Ere they could tell
This one was for you Jack
A promise we kept
This one was from mankind
It was for you we all wept

A M Stemp

SELFISH CENTURY

While man allows man to starve
In a world of plenty
While he allows people to sleep in doorways
When houses lie empty
Where children are abandoned by
Reluctant mothers,
Who could be in the arms of others,
Desperate to have a child, denied.
Waiting with their arms open wide.
While we avert our eyes
When people are mugged in the street
We do not go forward, we only retreat.
Will the next hundred years
Be better than the last
Can we learn from the hundred
That nearly have passed
How many of us have realised
We have no right to call ourselves
Civilised.

Heather Kirkpatrick

WORLD AS ONE

Together we must stand
The world as a whole
To look at the problems
And set up some goals.

We've damaged the world
with our fights and our wars
Destroying the forests
by building more stores.

Disastrous events have shattered us all
Illness keeps spreading from one to more.
People who help to improve situations
Unfortunate events, leaves us unsure.

Together we must stand
The world as one.
Undoing the damages we have caused
Helping to mend the things going wrong.

Rebecca Murby

THE MILLENNIUM YEARS

The stars and legends have brought us tears,
Through the last Millennium years.
President Kennedy so cruelly shot
Always in our hearts and never forgot.
King George the Sixth has suddenly died,
The Queen is crowned in front of our eyes.
The War has come and brave men died,
Leaving their children and wives behind.
A Coronation mug was given at school,
Then the Jubilee with a silver spoon.
A Legend was born: Mohammed Ali,
He fought like a butterfly and stung like a bee.
The Prince has found a wife to be,
The wedding was made for us all to see.
Prince William was born, a King to be,
But this we will have to wait and see.
The death of Diana, Elton did sing,
The emotional song: *Candle in the Wind.*
The Princess she will never be forgot,
For always in our memories and loved a lot.
What a Millennium we have had
Sorrow and joy, the good and the bad.

Dee Dickens

WORLD OF CHANGE

The twentieth century has brought about,
A world of plastic cards.
A situation not written about,
By our National-Bards.

No longer do we go around,
With pockets full of change.
In fact we don't need money,
Don't you find that strange?

Now who would want a robot,
To prepare and cook their food?
So I don't think this progress,
Is really for our own good.

Once it was enough,
To have qualifications by the score.
But if you haven't learned about computers,
No-one wants you anymore.

I think I'll keep my world,
Jogging along at a snail's pace.
I'll forget about this progress,
And the rest of the Human Race.

M Muirhead

ECSTASY

I looked at them. What could I see?
Their glamour replicated. A younger version of me!
I smiled. An older woman's reflective sadness
As they paraded, in today's fashion glad-rags.

They smiled to each other as I passed by.
Nudging, winking, brushing long hair from their eyes.
Little did they know on seeing me
That years ago, I thought I was like them, the total . . . Bees Knees.

They glazily smiled at me again. Then I could see
On drugs they were high. Probably Ecstasy.
What a sad sight and what a sad state
That illicit drugs, have sealed their fate.

Those beautiful girls, off-spring of my children's generation
Laughing at early death, with no hesitation.
The much prized grandchildren from their womb
Lost forever . . . in the New Century's tomb.

F S Fell

CHIMES OF TIME

Hear them shout, all about
The Millennium that is approaching
For the whole world the bells will ring out
The heat will definitely be scorching

But what of the past we leave behind
Will our future be any brighter
Or will our society still be blind
And wish for the majority to become quieter

Our world is scarred by so much pain
Such greed has all but consumed us
What do we all hope to gain
Let's hope it's acceptance and trust

A wonderful land for our children to grow
Is surely a much better reward, but
For things to change new seeds we must sow
Progression and positive steps forwards

The end of the century draws so near
And the tragedies are countless
We must stop the pain and fear
If we choose to fail, life would be pointless.

Lea Potter

A Century Moves On

This century is nearly up and I've been here for half
the changes that have taken place, do really make you laugh
With credit cards and cash machines, mobile phones and fax
We're ruled by numbers and IDs - there *is* no going back

Remember when the living costs never really moved
It stayed the same year in, year out, on petrol, fags and booze
The Government decided then to upset all the nation
By changing all our money round - they called it *decimalisation*

They're bringing down the barriers and integrating races
The melting pot bubbles on and on and spreads to far off places
We're all trying more than ever to get on with our brother
It's not easy - it never is - to live with one another

The world has really shrunk so small in the past 100 years
With Concorde at the speed of sound breaking down frontiers
We truly cannot keep this up - this never-ending race
The best place surely for this speed is up in outerspace

What's in store for the future? - It's difficult to tell
Will we be chatting by Internet and shop through it as well?
Will we fly to the moon for our holidays or even a day out
One thing for sure, all this technology, we just can't do without

I don't know if the inventions of the century
Are improvements or impediments to what we want to be
I know you don't need machinery and technological flare
To make the world a better place for people to live there.

Sylvia Kelly

THE FIFTIES

From the age of ten to twenty
The fifties were to me
A time of many changes
Too many to foresee.

At first when just a school girl
With friends at my side,
We'd laugh and just enjoy ourselves
As we went along life's ride.

I started work at fifteen
Then life changed for me,
Began to know how grown-ups feel
Can't wait to get my tea!

The days were hard but evenings fun
We'd meet and chat for hours,
About the things that all girls do
Boys, music, clothes and wedding flowers.

Then suddenly a major change
In love with heart a pounding,
Can't wait to see his face
Or hear his footsteps sounding.

I missed him when he went away
Wrote him letters almost every day,
We got engaged when he got leave
Became good friends with his family.

At almost twenty years of age
I married him, became his wife,
The fifties almost over in 1959
These years to me were a very *special* time!

Val Darling

NEW BORN FREEDOM

In a beehive-shaped mud hut with low door,
At end of the Great War, in South Africa
Nelson Mandela born to third wife of four,
Lived, barefoot, clad in blanket dyed ochre.

When five he guarded sheep and calves in fields,
On Sundays nurtured in the Methodist Church.
Men worked away at farms and mines with best yields.
He trained in university research.

With a friend he switched to Johannesburg,
Working as articled clerks in law firm;
Living in tin-roofed shack cold as an iceberg;
He learned about poverty in first term.

Qualified with his bachelor's degree,
His life was crippled by grisly racist law.
From a thousand affronts he joined ANC,
Pledged to freedom for blacks, their rights restore.

National Party's slogan Apartheid,
Kept blacks without vote, the white man always boss.
Mandela fought hard for his people's birthright.
Imprisoned for life, yet not all was loss.

With strong convictions he had time to think,
Knowledge is the enemy of prejudice.
Offered freedom if he broke guerrilla link;
Replied 'Justice for all with no malice'.

Following ten thousand days in prisons,
Mandela won his case for free election.
Voted President he hailed all citizens,
'At last we have gained emancipation.'

James Leonard Clough

THE ROCKING CHAIR

The old lady shuffled forwards
to her rocking chair.
She loved to sit and watch
the world go by from there.

Backwards and forwards the old chair
rocked in a steady way.
Her mind and heart still
so much alive even if old,
one hundred years and a day.

Reflecting over past years
to the days of long ago,
days of horses and carts,
a world where the pace seemed slow.

Where man and the earth were at one
and people would stop and pass the time of day.
They are in too much of a hurry now
as they wave, and rush past on their way.

To the sound only of birds
she sat there all alone
deep in her thoughts.
Of her sons and daughters
who from the nest had flown.

To Lionel in the Air Force
as handsome as could be,
to young Reuben and cheeky Joe
still serving in the Army.

Cheerful Amanda with
her little tribe of three.
Hannah the beauty
of the family.

Patricia G Gray

HOW COULD IT HAPPEN?

How could it happen?
How could you go?
When so many people
needed you so.

The newsreel was graphic,
depicting the crash,
A tunnel in Paris -
surrounded by press.

But back home in England,
in stunned disbelief,
the nation was silenced -
consumed by their grief.

We watched as the coffin
came off from the plane.
We saw shots of Diana
again and again.

Relentless as ever -
the media and press,
as the long week ebbed forward,
till she was laid to rest.

The lessons we've learned here,
we must never forget.
There will be no-one like her -
this century or next.

Linda I Willis

ONE HUNDRED YEARS OF PROGRESS

One hundred years have passed
And what a time it has been
Two World Wars, aeroplane flight, the car, television
And these are only a few of the things we have seen.
Man has travelled to the moon
The nearest planets they will come soon,
We have found cures for lots of diseases
But doctors still cannot cure the cough or the common sneezes!
We can travel in Concorde at supersonic speeds
We have even invented chemicals to kill off all the weeds!
But we still have poverty and hunger by the score
Maybe one day we will find compassion
To help the worlds hungry and the poor.
We have increased mankind's life span to seventy years and more
If we increase it to a hundred, will life itself become a bore!
If I could go back into time I wonder where it would have to be
For during the last century
There have been so many wondrous things to see!

J Barnes

ONE HUNDRED YEARS

Steam trains puffing along a country track,
Men on horses looking forward and back,
Fields of flowers made into houses,
Beautiful woods changed into motorways,
Hundreds of days are now gone,
Hid behind memories and photographs,
Families who live through wars,
Smile and wonder at the kitchen door,
Children dance across a hundred years,
To a land where computers and education,
Is the rally call, for all.

Kenneth Mood

SKY-WAY KNIGHTS

For a moment watching, all is at peace
In the golden Cornish countryside,
Sweet cool breezes, fan our faces
Uplifted, expectant excited.
We wait for the sounds of challenge
From twenty-six men, shoulder to shoulder,
Friends, mates, brother, companions
Determined to excel at Fincastle.
Fiercely proud maritime airmen, descendants
Of warriors and sailors, brave pioneers,
Charge their throbbing engines
As growling, rumbling and roaring, silence shatters.
Vibrant and powerful, compelling our attention
A metal chorus rings out,
The battle cry to other air-crews
Silver might streaks down the runway.
'St George for ever', emblazoned on our hearts
We cheer, our pride in noble blood consuming,
Enveloping, other airmen stepping out from time
To salute their comrades, then departing.
Champions all, the past and present mingling
Pacific and Atlantic, Sky-way Knights,
Soar upward, born of man and spirit
Climb smoothly, through the heavens wide.
Welcome the sun of a new dawning
Century, embracing nations from Commonwealth grown,
Theirs the hand of friendship freely given
In courage, at Fincastle on patrol.

Cynthia Beaumont

PROGRESS!

Always open, when passing by,
      colourful displays to catch one's eye.
Musical chimes if I opened the door,
      sweet smell of pine, on daily washed floor.
Cheerful smile from familiar face,
      service a pleasure, never a race.
Always remembered even by name,
      'how are the family', a well meant refrain.
Old fashioned tills (not robot controlled!)
      items hand-priced, without any bar codes.
'Do you have . . . goods' were always . . . 'somewhere' -
      unearthed in a rummage, and wrapped with care.
Well stocked shelves would have all your needs,
      from groceries, sweets, to soap, candles and seeds.
Magazines, books, cards, newspapers, sold,
      buckets and mousetraps, even ice-lolly moulds!
A little oasis, in backwater street,
      a chore made easy, to buy was a treat.
Then everything changed with new 'Superstores',
      takings fell low, outdone in price wars.
Now boarded and shuttered, and empty within.
      I ask of myself, who bears the sin?
For though I see progress, I feel we *all* lost,
      in failing to use, - a small corner shop.

Renée Halford

In Times To Come

How I love to run around
On England's finest grass,
And listen to the singing birds
Whenever trees I pass.

How I love the smell of leaves
When they are damp with dew,
And the buzzing bumble bees
When they have work to do.

How I love the sky at night
Its full moon high above,
When each star winks at you in turn
With promises of love.

How I love the riverside
When all is still and calm,
To watch the water pass me by
And lose all track of time.

All these things I love to see
To touch and to enjoy,
I wonder if, in times to come,
These things we'll not destroy.

Theodosia Soteriou

FROM END TO END

The century began one hundred years ago
Where it has gone I do not know
Our lives have changed some would say
For the better day by day.

So let us recall when it all began
Way back then if indeed we can
When people lived such simple lives
When husbands were husbands and wives were wives.

When children could play in the street without fear
There was no danger of them being there
When pony and trap was the people's way
For getting about day by day.

There were no gadgets for their daily toil
From washing the clothes, to tilling the soil
Everything was done by the worker's hand
By woman at home and men on the land.

The times were hard, but people knew
How to join forces, to see things through
When the wars were with us we rallied round
We looked after each other and friendship we found.

When the men were away for years on end
If we were strangers we soon became friends
Through all those years things have progressed
It's been a lot for us to digest.

But by and large we've seen it through
It's advanced the minds of me and you
As the century ends we wait to see
What the next one brings for you and me.

Edna Adams

MANKIND

Mankind has progressed so much
Over the last 100 years or so
The things we have learnt
That once we didn't know.

We have learnt to fly
With the invention of the plane
Which can take us anywhere
And bring us back again.

We have learnt to drive
With the invention of the car
Which means we can travel
Either near or far.

We have learnt to communicate
With the invention of TV
Bringing the rest of the world
Into the homes of you and me.

We have learnt to look beyond
With the exploration of space
Which hopefully will benefit
The entire human race.

But it won't mean a thing
If we can't live together
For it will all be irrelevant
If mankind disappears forever.

Ian Fowler

OUR NEW CENTURY

When the third Millennium begins,
Let a blessed star's covenant,
Start from within;
With thoughts, love and happiness free from sin,
The past years with wars and strife, now dim,
Lovely days with people, we loved and lost, sadly
Now gone with the wind.
Let thoughts of a kind nature be our theme;
Say a kind word and pray each day,
Our lives should become happier in every way.

Ethel D Smith

NO SHOES REQUIRED

Bare-foot kids all a-dancing,
On August pavements - hot.
Shoes for Sundays, or in winter,
For summer pavements, not.

Shoes for dancing, Charleston-style,
With every Bright Young Thing,
'Moving Pictures', 'Talkies' too -
Get in the mood for 'Swing'!

Rock around the clock a-while,
Dig those rhythm 'n' blues,
High-heeled sneakers, and all that jazz,
Don't step on my blue suede shoes!

'Winkle-pickers' twist and shout,
With 'stilettos' making holes,
On the dancefloor where the 'Bovver' boots
Groove-it with the 'Platform-soles'!

History repeats itself,
'Foot fashion' is never new -
But where are the bare-foot children
Who could 'dance' without their shoes?

Janice Trueman

THE HANDS OF TIME

Tic . . . toc . . . tic . . . toc . . . a century says goodbye,
Tic . . . toc . . . tic . . . toc . . . the hands of time do fly,
And as it comes to a close,
Many tears will be shed,
For loved ones we have lost,
The things we should have said.

Two world wars took their toll,
Brave lives lost, so we could be freed,
Such courage now hard to understand,
In a world so full of greed.

Other heroes too, were taken in their prime.
President Kennedy, Elvis, John Lennon, Princess Diana,
Surely it wasn't their time?

But through all the adversity seen through the years.
Others have brought us hope through our fears.
Mother Teresa's kindness made us beam,
The music of the Beatles made us scream,
And the haunting words of Martin Luther King
Who 'Had a dream'.
To mention only a few.
Have given us inspiration to keep *going*, in all that we do.
We don't know what the future will bring!
But let the bells to the new Millennium,

Ring . . . ring . . . ring.

Joan Fowler

AN ODE TO JOHN SMITH, MP

Sleep soundly John Smith, your long battle's been won
You'll live now in peace, from your home o'er the sun,
We Scots have arisen, chains and shackles now shed,
No more be down trodden, no more blood to be shed.

With the help from your party, we've now won the right,
To govern our proud nation, with true Scottish might,
Like a snowball that's grown, we've shown our true grit,
Sleep peaceful John Smith, we will still be a Brit.

The Tories were scornful, when they lost all their power
The lords and the gentry, lost their smarm, became sour,
We Scots stood and were counted, for all of their scorn,
Sleep peaceful John Smith, their fight was forlorn.

No more to be sneered at, our pride's been restored,
We walk with our heads high, now the lion has roared,
Your friends Tony Blair, and the Scot Donald Dewar,
Will let you sleep soundly, now they've given us the cure.

Now people of Scotland, we've got freedom once more,
Don't squander your chances, govern wisely, be to the fore,
Use you wisdoms and strengths, instilled through our creed,
Wha's like us, damn few, and aw them are deid.

Sandy Laird

OIL SPILL

Another ship breaks up at sea,
And bleeds its cargo for all to see,
A thick black lake is spread for miles,
To kill all in its path but why?
Spreading like black treacle across the beach,
A disaster to wildlife who cannot fight,
The incredible monster from the deep.

Veronica Harding

SIGN OF THE TIMES

The human race has become exactly that;
Each person rushing around pursuing some objective,
No matter how many people, he destroys in his path;
Time is relative, attainment is the key,
Speed the master, targets to be met,
Before, someone else jumps in first.
This obstacle race is thwart with snags and predicaments,
Each addition growing in stature,
Leaving the recipient even more perplexed,
Trying to cope, accept his plight, process the problems,
Before the pressure becomes too extreme,
Causing a total breakdown.
The mind like a computer can only input so much data,
Too much and it will crash, producing gobbledygook and drivel.
The questions are, how and when do we stop this chaos?
Or do we simply carry on floundering,
Until the world becomes nothing more,
Than an anarchic, fray of commotion and insanity,
Leaving humanity in a totally confused state.

Amanda-Lea Manning

THE CENTURY

Thirty six thousand, four hundred days,
that's how many when our century's done.
And in all that time the sun still shines,
stars still burn and the night still comes.
My parents were born, the wind still blows,
man walked on the moon, the world is in strife.
My father died, my child still grows,
in all that time, what did we do with life?
There's starvation, homelessness and in people despair.
Did we care . . . or not? When things got rough.
A computerised world with no feelings to share,
we achieved so much, yet achieved not enough.

Teresina N Fullard

TWENTIETH CENTURY TRUTHS

I brought you all this, and I gave you more,
You know what I'm talking about, you know the score.
The stars in the sky, they belong to us,
The birds and the bees, they're ours, no fuss.

You asked for these gifts, I gave without thought.
You planned for your death, you boasted, you fought.
So now don't look back and tell me you're proud,
Because yesterday's shawl is tomorrow's shroud.

I gave you the facts, placed clean on a plate.
I told you have patience, you just couldn't wait.
Well look at yourselves and then answer me clear,
Do I deserve your respect or do I get fear?

The science, the weapons, the dreams and the hopes,
The film shows, the heroes, politicians and popes.
World wars, football scores, distant shores and wealth,
Starving millions, men with billions, regardless of their health.

TV screens show ancient scenes, networks spread like fire.
Ad-men in their pin-stripe suits sell you your desire.
As one new cure is found for ill another life is saved,
As ancient wisdom dies alone the world becomes depraved.

We've come so far together, surely you must ask,
For guidance in the future, to help you with the task.
For though I may be older, and immeasurably more wise,
You, my child, are innocent, the future's yours, now rise!

Donald V L Macleod

DARK SKIES OF WAR

Oh for a glimmer of the summer sun
Thro' darkening clouds of gloom
The days of summer will soon be passed
It is now the last days of June,
And I have not seen a butterfly
Or heard the dull buzz of the bee,
Or bathed in the warmth of nature's fire
As summer days used to be.

The sky is filled with barrage balloons
To ward off Hitler's Hun,
We hear the wailing of the sirens
To tell us all hell has begun.
But we carry on working as before
And dancing the night away,
For we are all determined
Not to let Hitler have his way.

And when comes the dreaded telegram
From OHMS we regret -
We cope, feel sorry for the postman
Who has many to deliver yet.
We can tell our grandchildren, while we lived,
Many died to save their world.
And just hope, they'll grow up strong enough
To keep the flag of peace unfurled.

A Ferguson

20TH CENTURY (INVENTIONS)

When we recall the 20th Century with attention,
Surely we must remember man's invention,
The Wright brothers gave us flight,
And then there was radar, to see at night,
Submarines and other machines,
Cloning sheep from genes,
Then there was the cinematograph,
Charlie Chaplin made us laugh,
Wars brought machine guns and tanks,
And now we collect our money from automatic banks,
Food stored in tins,
Litter stored in bins,
The latest washing machine,
Helps to keep us clean,
Cars take us everywhere,
Concorde flies into the air,
Hoover's Hoover up the dust,
Cars are fixed with rust,
Edison gave us the phonograph and telephone, electric light,
Zebra-crossings - black and white,
And now man looks forward to the stars,
They're sending probes to Jupiter and Mars,
Lasers and phasers,
Rubber erasers,
Fleming found penicillin,
Logie Baird discovered television,
So who do we thank for all these great inventions
As we view the 20th Century with attention,
One answer:-
- God -

Alan Pow

THE APPROACHING MILLENNIUM

We approach the Millennium and look back with awe!
A single lifetime would not fill the score!
The law of sex discrimination has waved goodbye
Now that women clergy and astronauts reach out to the sky!

A change to decimal coinage from pounds, shillings and pence,
At present single currency is on the defence
New government tries to bring devaluation about,
'United we stand, divided we fall' why not all give such a shout!

We remember Chernobyl the Russian nuclear plant
Devastation covered the land, the animals, the peasants,
Global warming was recognised, an unusual planet seen in the sky
Observed by scientists with persistent eye!

An age of technology, improvements to the limit
Computerised subjects, knowledge and art within it,
Used in schools and offices today, and like a right-hand arm
It is here to stay!

We thank the Lord for fifty years of peace, yet civil wars increase!
The Irish situation, with discussions of peace, we pray indeed for
their release!
An 'Alpha' and 'Omega', a beginning and an end,
The light shines on a cross, to which everyone should bend!

Mary Dearnley

MEMORIAL

Stones underfoot indent the soles,
The beach awaits the pebble dash to the sea,
Gulls wheel and deal on high
In frantic round,
Whilst the sound of halyards
Snaps into the skies.

Prancing promenade preeners move in slow motion
As peel-back bathers drown in an ocean of lotion,
The sea heaves under fat, full-bellied spinnakers
Rounding the point just by Fort Gillkicker,
Thrill-seeker surfers take their rides on the rolling tides,
Under ice-cream clouds the crowds dispel and swell
As the Bay casts its spell.

Stones underfoot indent the souls,
The beach awaits the silent march from the sea
Of those who left this shore for foreign lands
To fight and die with honour on those beaches,
That we might with our children play and savour
Those pleasures yet unknown and still untasted,
That we might have this day
Along the Bay.

S Davies

STOP THE FIGHTING, SHOW WE CARE!

Take a look at the world we live in
We have civilians fighting for turf
Due to the failure to communicate
We have no peace on earth.

A civil war we do not need
With so many lives in hand
The brainwashed soldiers fighting hard
For their promised land

For the love of God we should not fear
In the minds our memories store
Our friends and families that we love
Why we are still at war

Is this the life that we should lead
When we have peace and love to share
For the world is one big family
Stop the fighting, show we care.

For the pain and suffering we see each day
To the riots and traumas we hear
We put on a smile to walk on the streets
As we battle our own inner fear

We the people today we seem to forget
Why God gave us this world
Let peace and love before us
And make an effort, make us proud

For this is the life that we should lead
As we have peace and love to share
For the world is one big family
Stop the fighting, show we care!

Steven Tanner

TODAY...

Constant shores are shifting,
  Poles' ice begins to melt,
There's sign of global warning,
  How is nature to be dealt
We've tower blocks,
  And express trains,
You can fly on Jumbo jets,
  Cruise on ships across the sea,
Join the Common Market
  Helicopter ambulances
People rich and poor,
  Traffic jams on our roads
Motorways galore,
  Rapid changes in our lives
As we go from day to day,
  Pollution in the air we breathe
What more can I say,
  Friends of the Earth and Greenpeace
Recycle of paper and tin
  Saving our forests and waters
Stop animals becoming extinct
  We must all unite together
Save our world in which to survive
  For this is our children's future
A good reason for being alive.

E Jones

MILLENNIUM

'Ring out the Old
. . . Bring in the New'

Lay the ghosts from the past
And leave them behind where they belong

Take your destiny in your own hands
. . . Have courage
And with determined steps
. . . Walk on into the light

Shatter the mirror of illusion
. . . Become part of the reality this night

Stand from the crowd
Let your voice ring loud

Search within yourself
. . . And be
For this is your beginning
. . . You are free

Accept the challenge
Seek the glory

'For when you die
No one else will tell your story.'

Sheila Peacock

FOR BETTER OR WORSE?

Soon the twentieth century will be gone and behind
The start of a new century. Perhaps of a different kind.
So many new things that have come along
The past generations we knew be history and gone.
Could peace ever come with the countries at war?
Or do we go back in time as it used to be before
In the earlier times of this century now past
Could we make the peace that will eternally last.
Many more great discoveries will be created
Perhaps to bring better. Perhaps to be fated.
Yet who is to find, we may not be here to know
For we be the older generation. The young are to grow.
Could these young ones mature to create a new life
Will there be such a thing as husband and wife?
Times have changed in such an unusual way
Sometimes we don't understand what young ones say.
Could eventually there be no such thing as work to go to?
Perhaps no reason now, for these machines it all can do.
How will one earn money, with no employment about
Could this then be the beginning of another war to break out?
Destiny is money that everyone needs for
With no work - no home, again it could only bring war
Theft and damage done for money, whatever the last hope
To somehow achieve money that man needs to cope.
Could this be the last century restarting again?
All that was discovered no longer be a future gain.
So many questions that are to be yet uncovered
What will life become, when this fate is discovered?

April Denham

ODE TO A CENTURY

As we leave this century
What changes have we seen
A turnover in the monarchy
With at least three kings and queens

A man on the moon
And planes in the sky
Hot-air balloons
Who said man can't fly?

The Titanic disaster
Its very first trip
So many lives lost
On that infamous ship

And then Britain at war
With food held on ration
Making rich people poor
With no money for fashion

Those brave suffragettes
Stood up for the right
To vote with the rest
And then won their fight

But what will we find
In the next hundred years?
I don't really mind
As I won't be here!

Ruth Sutherland

A Sign Of The Times

The place feels safe when it's sunny and bright
calm and serene by day.
The place is scary and troublesome by night
and you make certain to hide away.

People smile in daylight hours
and take children and dogs to the park
but shadows at nightfall
bring warnings to them of the
dangers that lurk in the dark.

A small estate of poverty and crime
makes people afraid to be out
Is this just a sign of the times?
Is that what it's all about?

The night-time shadows bring gangs
and thieves and drug-takers
litter the park, youths are fighting
and stealing cars;
A nice place by day but nasty come dark.

A child throws a ball to a dog by the lake
children see swans and bread they take
by day this estate is buzzing with life
but at night the air could be cut with a knife

A place full of crimes
or a sign of the times?

Pamela Smith

MILLENNIUM

The year 2000 is growing nigh
How the years soon pass by,
Is it me, now I'm getting older
That the winters seem so much colder?

The things that happened since I was born
They thought it great when they climbed the 'Matterhorn',
Then they put a man on the moon
Everyday travel in space available soon.

There's computers and faxes, Grandad wouldn't believe
There's helicopters, Concorde, and satellite dishes pictures receive,
Mobile phones to carry in your pocket
I don't know how they work without a socket.

Compact discs, stacking systems, that spoil the decor
No more LPs or 45s not anymore,
The days of the bin men have nearly all gone
Now an automatic arm that even puts the lid back on.

Radiators in offices and homes that made us soft
Six-inch wrapping up in the loft
All of these things our life to improve
Maybe I'm the one stuck in a groove.

But don't think for a minute I'm not vastly impressed
At some of the things they've done in the past,
Like ferries that go from Dover to Calais
You're on, then off, with no dilly-dally.

All of these things our life to improve,
But cloning of 'Dolly' I do not approve,
What comes next I'm not sure I want to know

So when the century ends let the party begin
Bring out the vodka, the rum and the gin,
Let's all be thankful that we are still here
And drink a toast to the following year.

Felicity Pigtails
REMEMBER

Remember, remember,
when I was young,
the winters were shorter,
the summers were long.
When I was young and full of play
Where were you then?
You had gone away.

All I can remember of my childhood days,
the skipping ropes, the spinning tops.
Around the lampposts we played.

If I could turn back the hand of time,
I would ask you to stay
because you were my dad,
and still you went away.

My heart was broken, it was broken in two
but after all these years gone by
I still love and remember you.

C Wilcock

PRECEDING THE MILLENNIUM

The twentieth century has to be the most progressive
                                        of all time,
So full of events both ridiculous and sublime,
The best of evolution since anything began,
The most important revolution in any time of man.
Man trying to fly like a bird is really number one,
Jumping off mountains, arms flapping, now that is gone,
Replaced by engine-powered planes of a different shape,
Making people stand in awe, with their mouths agape.
Going onto jet engines getting people away,
Travelling thousands of miles abroad in a single day.
Onto another kind of race,
Which country was going to be first in space,
Next I suppose I shall be visiting Mars,
Or holidaying on one of the cooler stars.

Another step forward was of course the car,
With an engine inside this could travel far,
With improved fuels to improve the thrust,
Meant higher quality designs became the 'must'.
With emissions from cars, other gases in the air,
The ozone going thin, looks like people don't care,
Diabetes stabilised, spare part surgery it seems,
Medicine has progressed beyond our dreams.
With wars that have happened, so many dead,
Lessons have to be learned, and kept in the head,
Life is never simply run by the letter,
But we must work out the problems to make life a little better.
Look forward to the millennium to learn new skills,
Finding new cures for lots of ills,
Getting a tolerance for people of all creeds,
Therefore sowing lots of Millennium seeds.

Patricia Baker

POETRY IN MOURNING

Poetry lies weeping for her children.
Mourning the loss of her alliteration,
In sorrow for the death of assonance.
And walking in unmeasured hesitation,
With feeble feet, she falters in the dance

The classic poets, sleeping now, at rest,
Whose words could pierce any hardened breast
are lost inside a most unseemly chatter.
But the World is not listening.

Instead of poets taking up the pen,
the banner has been grasped by others; then
within the sacred circles of their 'art',
they wield assassins' knives to great effect.
It's Poetry they're stabbing through the heart,
committing crimes that no one would suspect.
For people shrug, and say it doesn't matter,
as the World has stopped listening

Save other maniacs, who say they're better,
then follow that same nuance to the letter.
Lost in their fantasy of fearful need
born of a spate of avarice and greed,
to have their words inscribed within the scroll.
But modern odes have lost their erudition.
Such words may find their first, and last, edition
Meaningless phrases, soon to fade away,
in haste they're written, quickly they decay.

While Poetry lies weeping for her children,
in a World that's stopped listening.

Thomas Vaughan Jones

REFLECTIONS

It's time to reflect on the last hundred years
So much achieved through toil and tears
Who might have thought so long ago
Planes would fly high and low
And man could walk upon the moon
Cars on the road and hot-air balloons.

Two world wars with great loss of life
So much sorrow, heartache and strife
Pray for peace that it may last
So we will never be able to repeat the past
Compassion and love in abundance to share
For those lost in the world we must always care.

The old tin bath behind the door
Gas mantle on the bedroom wall
Boiler and mangle set in place
For mother to wash at a steady pace
The toil of washday gone for good
A machine takes its place where the old tub stood.

The wireless has gone, local radio's the thing
We've plenty of time to listen and sing
Computers and videos are all the rage
What will come next is hard to gauge
The oceans are sailed, the mountains they climb
Around the world in next-to-no-time.

Medical science a wonder of our age
So much technology written on every page
The heart and lungs can be replaced
Artificial joints put in with so much haste
The future looks bright for the young and old
So let's look ahead whilst the story unfolds.

Ann Mustard

THE TWENTIETH CENTURY

On the 20th century we see the signs of times
There have been rumours of wars and wars
That have taken many lives
In various places, famines and earthquakes
That makes one's heart quake
Nation rises against nation
And kingdom against kingdom
Among the young and the old
Because of the increase of wickedness
The love of most had grown cold
The Lord had told us ahead of time
False prophets and false Christ
Will appear and perform miracles and great signs.
Is the twentieth century the sign of the times?
If we look in the Bible, Matthew 24
We see the Lord's return is right at the door
And there is more, so much more,
The end of the twentieth century is drawing near
Are we ready for the Lord, or is there a lot to fear?
As we begin the third millennium
Where does one soul stand before God?
I'll leave you with that question.

Tanya Benton

TWENTIETH CENTURY

It's been a century of change for the human race,
first the horse and cart, now they travel in space.
People dreamed of flight in a plane,
it's become reality, no need to wish again.
To travel afar, by steamship we'd go,
now people use a submarine below.
Steam engines, they used to get us around,
who'd have thought it possible, to go underground
An open fire, so warm, so bright,
we have central heating, keeping us warm at night.
A television tube, brought pictures and news,
the silicone chip, makes a computer easy to use.
Once a simple line, the telephone's changed so much,
today they're portable, keeping us constantly in touch.
From the dance halls of some bygone age,
comes a disco for the modern days.
Gas or candles helped people see at night,
electric bulbs turn our darkness to light.
There's been two world wars, with much waste,
perhaps in the new millennium, we'll be a more tolerant race.

Chas Mowforth

WHAT HOPE THEN FOR THE MILLENNIUM?

Well how far did we get?
I know, it is not quite over yet.
But it seems to me,
That it looks pretty gloomy.
People still harm and kill people
And Government policies are feeble.
Babies and children are our heritage,
Yet, worldwide news coverage
Plots their misery and plight,
Neglected and starving, without a fight.
Or, Abused regularly in a civilised society,
Shows infant care is taken far too lightly.
What hope then
For the new millennium?
Is nothing learned from over-education,
Do we struggle to find a dedication?
And demand humanitarian solidarity
By broadcasting that every person is a rarity,
Deserving compassion and understanding,
Or is that just too, too demanding?
The past will remain,
Does the future have to stay the same?

Vivienne Doncaster

THE 20'S AT PLAY

When I was a child living in my day
We had seasons for each game we'd play.
There were several games with a bat and a ball,
Like cricket with stumps chalked on a wall.
We'd run along hitting a hoop with a stick;
For this game you had to be quick.
The game I liked was called 'Tip Cat'
Hitting a piece of wood with a bat
Seeing how far the wood did go,
Through someone's window with an unlucky blow.
Then came the turn of the skipping rope,
If you couldn't skip you were called a 'dope'
Our rope was the end of Mom's washing line
It had no handles, but it did us fine.
Then we'd play with a whip and top
Spin and whip the top till it stopped.
Our marbles we'd roll along the gutter,
Our hands got dirty but it didn't matter.
We were just hoping that we would win
But if we lost we would only grin.
Hop Scotch was another game
And win or lose 'twas all the same.
We all joined in and had lots of fun
Out in the air and in the sun.
I'm afraid the children of today
Don't really know how to play.
They only watch TV, or play a computer game,
But to me I don't think this is the same
As trying to win but to accept if we'd lose.
I know which era I would choose.

G Smith

BILL CLINTON - PRESIDENT OF THE WORLD!

The election grew near,
Competition was close,
Everybody questioned who would
Be, the right person for the post.

The day dawned,
Votes were cast,
Numbers were counted,
Then results at last.

Bill Clinton had won
The Presidential Seat,
With Al Gore as his Vice,
He adopted his feat.

His first four years in office
Proved him a true leader,
He aided peace-processes worldwide
Portraying him a succeeder.

So for a second term in office,
Clinton once again campaigned,
And won with a landslide victory,
Through all the votes he gained.

It was clear that he was the right candidate,
For the most powerful job in the world
President of the United States of America,
The forty-second and forty-third.

He takes an interest in all people,
Nationality, race and creed,
In the environment - preventing landmines,
And attempts to save countries from poverty or greed.

So Bill Clinton will remain,
For the White House and for me
This century's favourite President,
Now, and always in the future to foresee.

Lorraine O'Shea

DIANA

It is hard to think of anyone better
over the past 100 years who was such a 'go-getter'.
It was indeed Diana, Princess of Wales,
who brought such joy and happiness throughout her short years.

She was the voice of the people who looked to her for help
and her presence by those in power was certainly felt.
She was patron of many charities who now miss her smiling face,
but she lives on with them in spirit, even though there is

an empty space.

Her two sons were her life and she loved them dearly,
but there were times when all, did not seem too clearly.
However, her life changed, and she no longer seemed fraught,
as radiant she looked, aboard her friend's yacht.

But unknown to us all, it was soon going to end,
an accident in Paris, killed Diana and her friend.
A cloud hung over the world on that day,
but as the weeks passed by, it slowly drifted away.

Now the sequence of events seem so hard to understand,
that someone so kind-hearted who cared without demand,
should have such a tragic end to such a young life
so bedevilled and torn by words and strife.

She will never be forgotten as her memories will always be there,
carried with great dignity into the 2000th year.

Margaret Brown

SRI LANKA'S LIONHEARTS - THE WORLD CHAMPIONS

*(Dedicated to the Sri Lankan team who defend
the World Cup title in 1999)*

The thud of leather on willow, the lines were drawn,
the battle was well and truly on.
A sea of lions in red and yellow fluttered by,
as the excitement and expectations rose to new heights.
The figures in blue were smiling on the field -
eager, confident, brave lionhearts on centre stage.
The proud Australians were in a spin,
a hesitant mass in yellow trapped
in front of the uncompromising wickets.

The came Jayasuriya and Kaluwitharne, skittled,
disappointment etched indelibly on their faces.
The dependable Guru strode out
lashing sixes with fiery aggression.
The mighty Aravinda batted with eloquence and style,
stubbornly defending the prized wicket,
driving his way into the record books -
with membership in the Centurion's Club,
alongside Richards and Lloyd.

The cool, calm and collected Ranatunga -
Lanka's captain scored the winning run.
The crowd went wild, the boys in blue ran amok
As Arjuna and Aravinda hugged each other,
a symbol of teamwork and the Captain's steady rudder.
The countrymen wept tears of joy,
numbed by the sudden realisation -
the impossible had been achieved in Lahore.
The lion roared with delight - Sri Lanka had won the fight.

Ivan Corea

RAMSEY'S TROUPERS!

England's soccer heroes;
Wembley, '66;
World War II, relived, again
With football's, magic kicks!

The triumph of the century
As far as sport, extols;
With fighting spirit
To the end
And quadruplet of *goals!*

It Hitler left
When, Jesse Owens
Won the hundred yards;
He'd have had - a fit
As England's Boys
Excelled - as, *Soccer's bards!*

Kevin Setters

SIR WINSTON CHURCHILL'S STATUE

An effigy so powerful
Of a man does tell
Hard he worked
And hard he schemed
To serve his country well
Sir Winston Churchill's watchful eye
His statue did portray
Overlooking Parliament
In no uncertain way.

Melvyn Roiter

JOHN WINSTON LENNON
(1940-1980)

Sgt Pepper inspired love's march
Installing happiness on lonely hearts
Give peace a chance in '69'
Classics produced through fragile hands
Instant Karma will get you
Lyric's painfully truthful
Distance steps clearly set sail
Imagine settlement across ocean waves
New York City sounds fine
New-born arrives, form of Beautiful Boy
Blink goodnight through innocent eyes
Sudden death
Darkened Manhattan's light
John's memory peacefully bright.

Alan Jones

POEM OF THE CENTURY

It is nearly the end of the present millennium.
After the year 2000 a new century will come,
And as we approach the end of this decade
Let us stop and think of the progress made.

Reflect on how mankind has shaped the past,
With wars, religion; and cars that go fast;
Rockets launched, aiming for outerspace;
Phones and faxes, computers with interface.

Remember the famous names that have come and gone
While over us all the Sun steadfastly shone.
Politicians; actors and singers; the Arts;
A dazzling Princess, the Queen of our hearts.

What have we learned in the last thousand years
That we can take with us, to allay our fears
Of crossing into the unknown and unseen
Where none but Star Trek has as yet been.

Let us not forget the wars, but start no new strife,
And use our technology for a much better life.
Let us welcome new times and all work as one
And make Mother Earth shine back at the Sun.

Janis Old

TWENTIETH CENTURY GREATS

As I think back to the 1960s
And '61, the year I was born
I can unfold so many memories
Of the 20th century, I'm proud to have known
The Arrival of the Beatles
Paul McCartney
John Lennon
And Co
Not forgetting . . .
Neil Sedaka
Helen Shapiro
Mick Jagger
And all

Along came the 70s
Bellbottoms, platforms and Soul
Hello Maggie Thatcher
Goodbye Elvis, The Legend
Of Rock and Roll

In '81 Charles married Diana
Queen of Hearts she later became
Spreading love and warmth to everyone
A 20th century memory she will
always remain.

Denise Hemingway

MILLENNIUM

Inexorably the time will pass.
The century creeps away.
A page of history written up
as we have grown a day.

A new millennium is near
with plans and hopes and dreams,
and we may meet it at its dawn
along life's flowing streams.

When we look back, this century
will tell the whole of us.
Successes, failures, might-have-beens
and joys and grief and fuss.

Etched on the tree of life our lives
recorded, are so small,
yet there were days I cherished, when
my branches seemed so tall.

We'll see the imprint of our loves
as every new year starts.
Beginnings fondly in our minds
and endings in our hearts.

God called the ever-changing roll
and names and legends grew.
Though fame and fortune passed me by
the century brought me you.

I blinked. One hundred years are gone
in twinkling beams of light.
I look above and stars of love
will keep next century bright.

John Christopher

POEM FOR A CENTURY

People born in early nineteen hundreds
Who are still alive today
Can probably see that it's no longer
Work and rest and play.
These days not so many work
Most just want to play
To vandalise and mug our old folk
And have it all just their own way.
The days of give and take are over
They take but never give
Still keep on trying you never know
One day they may live and let live!

Joyce Matthews

UNTITLED

When we look back at this century
There were happenings too dire for eyes to see
We masquerade as a human race
atrocities were common-place.
Dungeons, torture, beheadings, not rare
We moved on a pace, but it's still there
The *holocaust* on a par with any
inhuman act gone before.
The killing fields more recently
Bosnia stripped away decency
But hope springs eternal as they say
So as we live in the present day
we must look back to later times
with men on the moon and the wonderful
inventions man has devised.
Penicillin, electricity, which gave us light
No more candles to burn at night
The car, the washing machine,
disposable nappies, to keep baby clean,
Computers now in many homes,
Calculators, the mobile phone.
As we race towards a new millennium
from the past we should be warned
Have the lessons it should have taught us
            Really and truly been absorbed?

Joan E Bartlett

A CENTURY AGO

My mind is wandering aimlessly
Listening to the chimes of the clock,
One hundred years by us
Like the time going by, tick tock, tick tock.

Buildings are getting higher
Pollution is at its peak,
A Royal lady we have lost
Is the future looking bleak?

Christmas is still in December
The queue in the traffic is always slow,
Seasons in summer and winter
We wait patiently, then they go.

Too many things to remember.
So much we shouldn't forget
Remembrance Day in November
And another month is set.

A disaster, a triumph, they're all words
                              we have used
To describe an event taken place,
Some have lost their loved ones
A tragedy they can only face.

Will we ever look at things the same
As we challenge a new century to come in.
But we must preserve the past
And all that is gone will be missed.

Cheryl Watson

THE 20TH CENTURY FAMILY

The twentieth century has plenty to boast,
Advance in technology has surprised us the most.
My new fitted kitchen, makes light work each day.
Whatever would Grandma and Great Grandma say!
With dishwashers, freezers and gadgets galore -
What new inventions do we have in store?

Remember we washed in cold water at dawn,
Now running hot water, greets us each morn.
Modern housekeeping has taken a new look.
We no longer refer to Mrs Beeton's cookbook.
The need to relax is always so great;
We constantly rush, for fear of being late.

There is television, video and plenty of sport.
To help us switch off, at least that is the thought.
These help us relax and escape our anxieties,
For stress is a symptom of the nineteen nineties.
So which do you prefer, to strengthen your heart
A workout in a gym or a walk in the park?

Travel at one time was only for the rich.
Cars, trains, ships or planes, they could choose which.
As a family we enjoyed an annual treat.
A coach trip perhaps or a day at Brighton beach.
But nowadays families holiday abroad.
Which reminds me of something that can't be ignored.

Family values should be maintained.
From being apart, nothing can be gained.
A musical evening, a storybook read,
That is the way to prepare for bed.
So the twentieth century has progress to boast,
But caring for families, matters the most.

Caroline Lester

POEM FOR A CENTURY

The years go by
The years unfold
Each New Year a story to be told.
The wars, the famine
The heartbreak the strife.
This is a part of everyday life.
The years of the cars,
The years of the planes
The years of the washer and
Dryer, man gains.
Man's intellect knows no bounds
But the world's become noisy
With all of these sounds.
Now we have the computer
The eye of Big Brother
The rocket has been to the moon.
Man forever far reaching
Sent a rocket to Mars
Man is now soaring up to the stars.

Margaret Whittaker

WHAT HAS THE 20TH CENTURY
EVER GIVEN US?

When I look back and ask the following question
What has the 20th century ever given us?
Here are some of the answers
War, famine, disease, disasters and droughts
Black and white gangster movies with
Cagney, Edward G and Bogart
Television BBC, ITV, Cable and Satellite
Rock and Roll, R+B, Heavy Metal, Soul, Pop,
Punk and New Wave Music
Holly, Stevie Wonder, Deep Purple,
Aretha Franklin, Bee Gees,
Sex Pistols, Adam and the Ants, Jam
and Spandau Ballet
Comedy greats, Tommy Cooper, Benny Hill
and Eric Morecambe
A galaxy of talent left us for heaven
Actors, actresses, politicians, artists,
musicians and Royalty RIP
Sports personalities, legends always live on
Atom bombs, nuclear weapons, electricity,
and the Space race
Also a man on the moon
Calculators, microwaves, stereo, microchips,
computers and compact discs
Scientific research, the Cold War, and the
three-day week Eurovision Song Contest,
decimalisation, Channel Tunnel and the M25
Other disasters include Cilla Black, Sinclair C5,
and double-glazing salesmen
England won the World Cup in 1966
with a Geoff Hurst hat trick
They think the 20th century is over
It is nearly.

Neil Mason

WAY AND THE LIGHT

An early occurrence recorded yet not proven as a lie
Such a bright starry light seen in the dark of a night sky

Bring forth the three wise men who travelled from afar
This light recognised by them not as a comet but a star

Scorned much and regarded by many doubters just a fable
To Mary and Joseph Son of God born in a lowly stable

A Boy Child considered by others as just another waif
Only to those who had never been searching for a faith

My own eyes I have seen it twice this shining light so nice
I thought it would rush fast through the sky in a trice

But it was there speeding not so fast round the world's top
Every three thousand years scientists claim Comet Hale Bopp

Yet to me not so the appearance of this slow majestic light
Amazed enchanted open-mouthed in wonder I watched at night

Two thousand years ago Jesus was born under such a light
Three thousand years Egypt no record with all their might

This light has travelled millions of miles and from where?
I can only guess others claim to know and they would dare

Perhaps this light came and seen here to foretell a story
Not for our admiration and wonder of shining majestic glory

Sometimes human alternatives very difficult to accept or find
Difficult to see with such brightness we sometimes are blind

Just observing I found heart and peace in the dark of night
I think by remembering Jesus said 'I am the Way and the Light.'

It could be such a bright light shining to herald a new way
With the forecasting of the coming of another special day

After seeing with my own eyes such a sight with no telescope
Nobody will convince or tell me otherwise . . . *There is hope.*

James Burns-Swan

LIFE'S PERFECT DAY

Birds singing, squirrels hopping
People running, flowers blooming
Water spraying, children laughing
The air is still the sky is blue
A perfect day to sit and dream
I dream of life ahead
I hope life changes for the best
I pray my dreams come true.

Janet Childs

WAR

The war is sad, the war is bad,
Lots of children lost their dads.
The memories of how life used to be
Before their daddies went out to sea.
Those flying machines flying high
Dropping bombs from the sky.
Lots of people running, scared,
Afraid their lives would not be spared.
Houses, buildings blown to the ground
Family, friends not to be found.
Lost and bewildered, feelings untold,
All they need are their loved ones to hold.
Although, victory was our gain,
We succeeded with great pain.

Maria Smith

A CENTURY!

A Century!
Of battles lost and battles won,
A Century!
Of princesses lost and princes gained,
A Century!
Of dreams and realities,
A Century!
Of mines planted and mines uprooted,
A Century!
Of lovers gained and lovers lost
A Century!
Of bitter hunger and starvation,
A Century!
Of child-labour and illiteracy,
A Century!

Of demonstrations and peace talks
A Century!
Of earthquakes and floods,
A Century!
Of life and death,
A Century!
Of farming and harvest,
A Century!
Of trials and tribulations,
A Century!
Of science and technology,
A Century!
Of failures and successes,
A Century!

Indeed a century to remember.

David Carvalho

LIFE THROUGH THE YEARS

Life has been traumatic
We've been through thick and thin
We should try and stick together
If we are to win
Many people need our help
To get through their troubled times
Countries that have disasters
Which cannot be explained
Why do they have to suffer? (There is no need)
Plane crashes, ships that sink, floods and storms alike
These things are sent to try us
To see if we can cope
So many things left unsaid, so many answers needed
Whys, wherefores, cries that go unheeded
Children needing parents, someone just to love
We all look for guidance from The Lord up above.

Nell Carruthers

THE LAW OF THE DESERT

A swish of a sword. Another man's hand
For the cost of a loaf, in burning sand
Lashes inflicted from a bamboo cane
Sharp metal across the neck, a slicing pain
A spurt of red blood, covers the sand
In the heat of a far off land
A deathly silence, a sickly hush
A torso falls into the dust
Hands are still tightly tied behind the back
A scream of terror, a man manacled to the rack
Rained blows down on naked flesh
Fifty or so leaves a gruesome mess
Dragged by four, to a darkened cell
Beaten, bloodied nearly dead, but still nothing to tell
A stench of death fills the air
But he vomits, as even for him it's too much to bear
His screams of anguish, for a mate now deceased
As hungry rats devour the feast
But all he dreads tomorrow, is the opening of the door
And all within a holy book, called the Koran which is the law.

Keith Regan

CENTURY'S SONG

We flew through the air, looking down to
Earth as if to say,
'At last, we've conquered you!'
We loved on sands and sang homeward
In jalopies where once we stayed home,
And even there those from outside
Touched us, and told us what they
Thought and made us laugh, cry or
Despair for them, as we watched them
Perform like puppets in a corner.
And when there were our private smiles and
Tears we could share them and let emotions
Pour as we spoke volumes through
Great rockets in the skies - that aren't
God's but ours, manmade.
This is how it started on a dream of love
And want; to speak through the middle
Air; winds; seas and lands, and learn to love again.
Then somehow the world went mad,
We spun around to realise if what we had was
More precious, than what we fought for?
For it was men who made these things,
The gadgets of time,
And the beloved we lost, as we sold them in war.

Sue Jackett

CENTURY, CENTURY

Century, century,
where do I begin?
So many events have
happened so quick.

Century, century,
do you fear?
Now that the end
is drawing so near.

Century, century,
you are reaching the end,
leaving many memories
of the living and the dead.

Century, century,
some received much pain,
whilst others have had
plenty to gain.

Century, century,
many shall pray to God
for the third millennium
to be very strong.

Century, century,
would you care to agree
that the future depends
on people like me?

Shabnam Yasmin

Poems For The Century

Two years from 1998 the year 2000, will be a new century
During the last 100 years, there has been many changes, certainly
Based in 1898 much poverty arose, the poor were getting poorer
With wealth, gold and silver, the rich were getting richer

Approximate, 60 years ago, if rents were unpaid, destitutes were
thrown in the streets
Come rain, snow or showers, there was frustration and defeat
Or, in the workhouse, poor society was getting worse
For the rich, more gold and silver possessions and money in their purse

When the war ended in the 1940's there was great victory
Rebuilding of buildings had to be finished, there was more sympathy
People were very friendly and helped one an another
Doors were left open, keys behind doors, possessions were safe
from the burglar

1960 - 1985 there were more factories, and miners, worked hard
down the pit,
Coal fires a light, more hospitals to choose from, for the sick,
There was humanity, churches open most of the day
That people could visit and share, perhaps a quiet prayer on the way.

People were safe to walk through the dark,
No snatching at handbags, wallets, even no fear in the park,
Through the late 1980's to 1997, there have been changes
and alterations
Redundancy, hospitals closed, pits finished, and more pollution

Throughout the new century, more changes may take place
For, God never changes, He who made the world from the beginning
of time, and space
He alone can give peace, and can work out the future
For, God is everywhere, and could see things change for the better

If we look up to God this very day, He will meet our need
There could be fairness, without poverty, in the future, indeed.

Jean P McGovern

Life - As We Know It

We are a people of many faces,
Our country, we share with many races.
We are a nation of great strength,
To help a fellow human, we'll go to any length.

In the face of adversity, we stand tall,
Like an indestructible wall.
The life we live determines our soul
Then destiny comes to take control.

In this world of never-ending pain and sorrow,
Will the millennium bring a new tomorrow.
Put your hands together in silent prayer,
To lighten the cross we have had to bear.

Place our hope in the next generation,
For they are our future and our destination.
They will go where wise men fear to tread,
And win this evil battle head to head.

Pat Vieyra

GET REAL

First there came the wheel,
Then the electric light,
Steam trains and ships,
Aeroplanes in flight.
But then there came the micro-chip,
A little thing compared to a ship,
And that's when Hi-tech stepped in,
Now we have computers, videos,
CDs and the talking bin.
But it's a thing that people rely on,
I liked it better when there was none,
Things where simple and they meant a lot,
We where thankful for what we got,
But the future goes on,
And we must get real.
But it's been a big step since the wheel.

Sylvia Mellon

YOU

I was still in the park
when the grass turned damp
and shadows grew long
before the sun set
below the darkening trees.
People had gone
but I lingered on
with the evening songs
of urban birds.
The geese streamed v-shaped
across a clear sky
that belonged to them.

When I wondered home
my heart was light
and full of stars.
I'd spent the afternoon
on a cloud
writing you a love song.

Mary Care

FROM TRAUMA TO TRIUMPH

The bells were silenced when the church burnt down,
   The people watched through the night.
How could this happen to God's own house,
   And to those who try to do right?

The fire-fighters came from all around,
   The vicar was roused from his bed;
They worked and they toiled, trying to put the fire out,
   And thanked God that no-one was dead.

They gathered around the ashes next day,
   Shocked, bewildered, dismayed;
They asked one another, 'What can we do?'
   And the first thing they did . . . they prayed.

And God in His wisdom came to their aid,
   And gave them the will to go on;
So 'midst sweat and tears, for days, months, and years,
   With the finest of builders . . . they won!

Now the choir leads the singing, the new organ is played
   For their praises to God, week by week;
And sightseers come from far and wide,
   For the splendour is there to seek.

The bells, in storage, are being prepared
   For the start of an inspiring venture;
The ringers eagerly await their return,
   To *greet a brand new century!*

Edith Cartwright

A TURN IN TIME!

Reminiscing I began; looking back,
Where history there stands still,
Reflecting England's glory,
Not to mention hidden scars,
Our victory of two world wars,
Devastating beyond words,
The long present reign of Elizabeth II
Throughout this century,
We have known many greats,
Of whom we had but a glimmer,
Although their parting brought great grief,
They were an inspiration to all mankind,
There is a reoccurring change-
Within the human race,
As time experiments with fashion,
Our confidence grows within our style,
Freedom of speech now paramount,
Progress is growing around the clock,
The triumph of flying of which -
Curiosity lead to the moon,
The glory of National Health,
At present almost dried out,
Life's discoveries - all very precious,
A moment of thought crossed -
On this turn of time - as the,
Third millennium approaches,
Remembering history - past lives,
Thee I dare ask myself -
What the future holds - for the world,
For England and mostly for *me!*

Karen Anne Nelsey-Brown

FOR THE MILLENNIUM

I've seen a coronation
Royal weddings births and death,
I've seen devastation
That war with Germany left.

As I grew up watched with wonder
Man's first trip into space.
Assassinations, inventions
And surgery on the face.

There's cures for this and cures for that
But one eludes us still.
There is no cure for cancer
Let's hope one day there will.

We've seen the war in Ireland
Its bloody battles still
In Bosnia and Middle East
Its never-ending ills.

Nutrition has got better
Life's quality has improved.
But we still have starving thousands
We still have a lot to prove.

So in the year 2000 the human race must work.
To make the world a better place
We're still feeling in the dark.
Man's attitude to man must change
We really must have peace.
We do not need the wars we have,
It all must end and cease.

K Pickup

LIFE

Why, only, and, if
I tell you people, this is not, a myth
Have belief, in what, you do
Explore your dreams, and follow it through
To the letter, to the name
Find yourself, in the book of fame
You've got to stride, for the very best
Yea, you don't wanna believe it, but it's like a contest
Everyone's, trying, to work it out
Don't give up the fight, don't have your doubts
Work yourself, to the top of the top
Don't wanna, be left, as wastage crop
Something, that, could have been
I've seen the light, I'm glad you've seen
Can you, really say, the world is yours
A statement, like that's, got to carry, a clause
Possibility, tour, all its floors
I think you'd find, there is, so many wars
The fighting, and, destruction, of man
I don't think, that was, God's plan
Got to release, yourself, get with the jam
Feel the vibes, go with, the flow
Move your body, go, go, go
Reachin', for, that destination
I tell you man, we're under, one nation
Penny, dollars, or even, pounds
Respect, goes out, to all you, on underground
These are, my lyrics, and that's a fact
I know where I'm from, and I know where I'm at.

Simon Peter Dennis

DUNBLANE

They had done no damage.
They had done no wrong.
They paid the price by being young.
Who knows? What's in someone's head, when they decide it all
must end.
In the wrong place at the wrong time, is no excuse for this
terrible crime.
Words cannot explain or actions replace the devastation of that
horrendous day.
Some tried to prevent the carnage, but all in vain and why? Dunblane.
Children who were born from love, struck down so quick,
nowhere to hide.
How much love died that day?
How many hearts just shrank inside.
We hope for the future and all the good things, but life can be cruel
with the sadness it brings.
Eternal thoughts for those who were wronged, helps us only to carry on.
There is no reason, so do not look.
Just believe in tomorrow and help others in life's storybook.

A Sackey

1940 WARTIME MEMORIES

Beyond the valley's silent hills
The echo of the past remind us still
Of another time
When dark clouds gathered
As the world was torn apart
The unleashed hand of evil
Then ran amok
Leaving within its path
Crumbling ruins
And cities of fire
As the lights went out
A raging storm
Was about to be unleashed
Upon a land
That once was a haven of peace
Burning deep within our troubled minds
The lasting memories
Of those terrible times
The harrowing nights
So often filled with constant fear
As the hand of evil
Drew closer, ever near
Time itself seemed to stand still
Beyond the valley's silent hills

A W Harvey

THANKS TO OUR ANCESTORS

A voice coming over airs,
People moving on a screen,
A cleaner taking away cares,
Washing done in a big machine,
Travelling fast in a racing car,
An aeroplane with shining wings,
Ships equipped with radar . . .
There are so many, many things -
All in this last hundred years,
When man has progressed beyond reason . . .
Some ideas allaying fears -
Changes it seems at every season.

Two wars brought us many sighs,
Thankfully we emerged safe and sound.
Between the nation's stronger ties,
Let's keep our feet upon the ground
And greet 2000 with a smile,
Ready to face it strong and true.
As we cover every mile,
Only our best will ever do.

Doris A Pearson

MEMORIES OF THE SECOND WORLD WAR 1939-1945

When deep in muse I ponder, recalling days gone by,
These wartime recollections appear in my mind's eye:-

The wailing, warning sirens with moaning, eerie cry;
The chilling drone of bombers high in the midnight sky.
The rush to air-raid shelters in gardens buried deep,
The air-raid wardens' vigils; the nights with broken sleep.
The black-out curtains hiding all trace of light indoors,
While searchlights combed the heavens, o'er cities; towns, and moors.
The ack-ack guns a-blazing with quick percussive burst.
Barrage balloons, grey, ghostly, afloat in cloud immersed.
Sandbags protecting buildings - they came in heavy loads.
All names of places vanished from signs along our roads.
For safety many children became evacuees;
To country homes they journeyed, or far across the seas.
Food rations seeming meagre, yet most of us survived -
We thought of loved one's fighting, so could not feel deprived.
And when short leave was granted, our hearts with terror filled.
The dread word 'embarkation' all other worries stilled.
We all knit socks for soldiers, warm gloves, and helmets too,
When wool was hard to come by, yarn mixture had to do.
We grew our own potatoes where flower-beds used to be,
And planted greens and lettuce - we 'dug for victory'.
All ornate iron railings were melted down for arms,
And girls joined the 'Land Army' to work on busy farms.
Hello-girls manned their switchboards, connecting urgent calls,
The ENSA concert parties performed in huts and halls.
Lord Haw-Haw on the wireless tried hard to undermine
Our staunch morale and courage. We scorned his plaintive whine.

For six long years war lasted, until the truce was signed
Pray God that in the future peace reigns for all mankind.

Eileen N Blackmore

1930-2???

I was born in nineteen hundred and thirty
No work, no food, no hope, just urchins, faces dirty
When a great depression swept the lands
A world war had just ended, rich men with blood stained hands
I went to school, read books, and learnt
While in Germany, books were burnt
Never went hungry, or felt the cold
And all was well, so we were told
But not for long, were we at peace
The depression and unemployment, would cease
For money can be found for war
And when that's gone, find some more
Hundreds of thousands of lives are lost
Must win the war at any cost
Money is no object, pay any sum
Then at last, the dreaded war is won
Austerity goes on and on for years
Rationing, and doing without, brings us close to tears
The shortages and the ever erupting wars
The constant struggle, to keep the wolf from our doors
We work hard, and have prosperity for a while
And all seems well, at last can give a smile
But the big bang comes, our livelihoods destroyed
People out of work, three million unemployed
But I wouldn't have lived at any other time
Even if the choice was mine
Not in the centuries before, or the centuries to come
The century in which I lived, for me, it was the one.

Keith Coleman

TWILIGHT 1955

Sheephatch in twilight, is Len Watkins awake?
Ghostly shadows are creeping through the brake.
Shadows of evening, dreaming in the dorm,
Dream a shadowy hill, over us till morn.

John Clark is here again, with his merry band,
To hear a cuckoo waltz, brighten up the land.

Bell, ring as before, loud and not far away,
In Sheephatch, in Sheephatch, at the break of day.

Happy, happy Sheephatch, in the month of June,
Sweetness the scent of flowers in their full bloom.

Carole Willmott and Sheila Locke are here again,
Jolly hockey sticks played through sun and rain.

A flight of butterflies fluttered in the mist,
Janet Barker's running with jewel of amethyst.

Happy, happy Sheephatch, awake as of old,
Tony Catherall paints you as bright as gold.

Miss Wheeler is here again, helping us to pray,
In Sheephatch, in Sheephatch, at the break of day.

Robin Pearcey

No Strings Attached

Perhaps an ambition of all of us is to be loved in some way by
everyone.
We know it makes the world go round and it's what soaps and
films rely on.
However, the meaning of love has been interpreted in many
different ways.
There are some who respect this, but the romantic element has
altered since the early days.
It should be the culmination of a friendship where two become almost
as one.
And with a lifetime of closeness have enjoyed every year that's come
and gone.
There are those less fortunate and unable to fulfil such a dream.
But love to them is still an essential, although there's no partner
in the scheme.
Here the love that can be exchanged with friends needs extra special
care.
It does not call for commitment or obligation - it's so very rare.
So although those on their own occasionally feel a close relationship
would be ideal.
There is love and friendship from so many that we know we can rely
on - and that is very real.

Reg Morris

TWENTIETH CENTURY

In 100 years we have gone far,
Wright's in the aeroplane, Henry Ford with the car,
King Edward VIII gave up his crown,
The Berlin wall went up . . . then down.
Emmeline Pankhurst got women the vote,
The world was conquered, single handed by boat.
Famine, disasters, the Titanic sank,
Band Aid and Live Aid put cash in the bank.
Elvis, The Beatles to name just a few,
Everyone tried to do something new,
Mountains were climbed, the sound barrier broken,
All of this a very small token,
Hurricanes, earthquakes and men on the moon,
The Twentieth Century will be memories soon.

Pauline Horsham

DECIMALISATION

Our money it changed
Everything re-arranged
We've all got to do something new.

New pounds and new pence
It doesn't make sense
What on earth are we going to do

Go back to school
Feeling the fool
I wish there was someone! But who?

To teach us to count
To know the amount
Of the money that we all get through

Hundred pence in a pound
Two coins that aren't round
At least the five pound note's still blue

The shilling is gone
The guinea's all done
This is to name but a few.

What's the value today
As we go to pay
It's hopeless! I haven't a clue.

Carol Duke

THE CANDLELIGHT VIGIL AUGUST 15TH '97

Thousands came to honour a man's name
on the eve of August 16th.
From all over the world fans young and old
lined up by Graceland gates to pay their respects.
Elvis Presley is that person
the candlelight vigil is the reason.
Never before have I seen such a sight
on a warm summer night.
There is no-one else in this world
who can command such love and devotion from his fans,
even though 20 years have passed.
As we walk slowly up the hill
to where time seems to have really stood still.
With love in our hearts and candles in our hands,
tears are in our eyes at the sight
of a grave with flowers, bears and cards piled high.
I was there to share in this historic event.
People queued for hours and hours in the heat
all along the street.
The police closed each end of Elvis Presley Boulevard
for the whole of the night,
so people can walk at their own pace and gaze at the sight.
If you're an Elvis fan you'll understand
what this is all about.
If you're not, don't mock, for no-one can stop
all this love we have for him,
he truly is our king.
He gave this world so much pleasure
that we all can treasure.
We must keep his memory alive forever and ever.

Helen Barrie

A CENTURY ENDS

A century gone.
Don't cut down the trees.
A century gone.
Less fish in the seas.
A century gone.
Fumes rising high.
A century gone.
A hole in the sky
A century gone.
Let's all reverse the trend
A century gone.
Put the Earth on the mend
A century gone.
Let's make some resolution
A century gone.
No more pollution.

J C Hall

DEAR DIARY

January 1st 1900

Oh, what a jolly time we had,
We stayed up late, I was so glad
To dance the waltz and sip champagne,
I'll relive last night again and again.

Mama had made me a brand new gown
In pink, with white lace running down
The front, then draped around the back
Caught with roses which she had to tack.

Then home in the carriage, snow on the ground,
The bells were ringing from all around.
We went then to bed, fun was had by us all,
Oh thank you, Papa, for my first New Year Ball.

Emma

January 1st 2000

Oh, what a brilliant time we had,
Stayed up 'til four, than I was bad.
I'd danced all night, drank too much champagne,
As I've said before - never again!

I'd been to the sales and bought a new dress.
I thought I looked cool, Dad said 'You're a mess,
Wear something longer and cover your chest,
I want my little girl looking her best.'

I crashed at my mates, lying on the floor.
I didn't sleep much, God she can snore.
We agreed that the guys didn't stand a chance
As we looked so smart at the New Year's Eve Dance

Emma

Sandra Sharp

WHY?

Oh! Those babies,
  How they'll be missed,
God will bless them,
  With his gentle kiss,
They'll play together,
  In God's playground,
Their baby laughter,
  A joyous sound,
Friends together,
  Side by side,
Their parents' hearts still,
  Filled with pride,
I did not know these little ones,
  But in my heart they'll be,
And for those heartbroken parents,
  I couldn't wish for anymore,
But peace and tranquillity.

Sue Turner

FUTILE TEARS

I've fought so hard throughout this long and solitary year.
I've felt the pain of infidelity, I've built a wall to conceal my tears.
For deep within my soul, I know our love is finally through.
It ended the moment I saw her holding and caressing you.

You will never know how much I truly cared.
I will never erase the memories of the seasons we both shared.
They are locked within my mind, at least she can't take them away.
I wish I could summon the courage to beg and make you stay.

Futile tears are now falling, for you have gone to her tonight.
You have placed her upon a pedestal, I guess it's time to concede
the fight
For your bitter-sweet loving and tender-warm embrace.
I will miss your carefree laughter, I will miss your sensuous face.

So when you decide to leave me, please don't say goodbye.
Don't look back or hesitate, I don't want you to see me cry.
For I've always been the strong one, and it hurts so much to
see you stray.
Alas, our love has turned to autumn, and with the leaves it's blown
away.
Now futile tears are falling.

Sandra Edwards

FORWARD

This century is drawing to a close
      In a year or two, or three.
What will the next one bring for us?
      We'll have to wait and see.

There's been quite a few Kings and Queens
      From Victoria, to the present.
There was an abdication too
      Which people did really resent.

Aeroplanes were invented,
      They were such flimsy things.
Now Concorde flies, at the speed of sound,
      Like a bird, with wind under its wings.

Rockets have shot into the sky,
      And man has been on the Moon
Men too have worked in outerspace,
      Will Mars be next? - Pretty soon.

This century has seen many wars,
      The Boer War, The Great, and The Second.
Korea, The Falklands, and Saddam Hussein's
      Only Death and Destruction, - I reckon.

Many great people have lived and died,
      Their daring and deeds remembered,
They made this Country as great as it is,
      Remembrance - November 11th.

Here's to the Twenty-first Century,
      What will it bring to us all?
Now raise your glasses, everyone.
      To the Millennium - let's have a ball!

Joan Smith

NINETEEN HUNDRED PART ONE

Long time ago in nineteen hundred,
Grave diggers did work night and day.
After a dreadful influenza epidemic,
took up to fifty people a day, away.
In London it was thus, at the beginning
of this industrious, new born century.
The other cities were hard hit too,
by this dreadful January flu.

Britain back then had an empire,
that almost stretched around the globe.
Though the Dutch peasants continued revolting,
was beginning to get up her nose.
Whilst in that fact, the Americans delighted!
Finding the Boer War, was good for trade.
Yet! They hated the Boxer rebellion,
and to the Chinese, an ultimatum made.

Before the year was out, gladly I say!
The Boer War had ended, many said 'In the best way.'
Yet Britain lost more than, eleven thousand men!
Though to the enemy only a third of them.
The other seven thousand mainly died of dysentery,
When the remaining troops returned triumphant! And
To vast processions, across the land.
Greeted as they were by the mayor,
Many of them must have felt,
Very lucky to be there.

L Dagmar Lee

INFORMATION

We hope you have enjoyed reading this book - and that you will continue to enjoy it in the coming years.

If you like reading and writing poetry drop us a line, or give us a call, and we'll send you a free information pack.

Write to :-
Poetry Now Information
1-2 Wainman Road
Woodston
Peterborough
PE2 7BU
(01733) 230746